CALL ME
LUCIFER

Dialogues with a
Noble Stranger

CALL ME
LUCIFER

Dialogues with a
Noble Stranger

EILEEN J. GARRETT

FOREWORD BY LISETTE COLY

Afterworlds Press

Santa Fe, New Mexico
www.afterworldspress.com

Published by Afterworlds Press; an imprint of White Crow Productions Ltd.

For information, contact White Crow Books by
e-mail: info@whitecrowbooks.com.

Cover image: Fallen Angel by Alexandre Cabanel
Cover Design by Astrid@Astridpaints.com
Interior design by Velin@Perseus-Design.com

Paperback: ISBN: 978-1-78677-192-6
eBook: ISBN: 978-1-78677-193-3

Non-Fiction / BODY, MIND & SPIRIT / Channeling and Mediumship

www.afterworldspress.com
www.whitecrowbooks.com

For Eileen J. Garrett, who spoke with wisdom to so many in this world and beyond, and continues to do so to this day.
—Lisette Coly

ABOUT THE AUTHOR

~

E ileen J. Garrett (1893-1970) was an Irish medium and one
of the most important figures in parapsychology. Despite
her apparent psychic abilities, which were subjected
to numerous tests by the most prominent researchers of the
era, Garrett maintained a lifelong healthy skepticism, always
questioning the nature and meaning of her own extraordinary
experiences. Her dedication to the objective, scientific study
of psychical phenomena resulted in her establishing the

Parapsychology Foundation, which published many books on the subject as well as the *International Journal of Parapsychology,* and the popular *Tomorrow* magazine. Garrett was also something of a *bon vivant,* rubbing shoulders with everyone from Sir Arthur Conan Doyle to Cecil B. DeMille, Aldous Huxley, Salvador Dalí, Robert Graves, Anaïs Nin, and Carl Jung to name but a few. Garrett herself was a prolific author, writing a number of novels as well as books on psychical research and three autobiographies – including *My Life as a Search for the Meaning of Mediumship,* available as a new edition from Afterworlds Press.

PRAISE FOR *Call me Lucifer*

"*Call Me Lucifer* is a fascinating account by Irish medium and parapsychologist Eileen J. Garrett of her life-long relationship with a personality that identified itself as Lucifer. Through her conversations with Lucifer – interpreted variably as a separate entity or an aspect of her subconscious – Garrett explored key issues of modernity, such as the Self, the subconscious, sexuality, and spirituality. As such, Garrett's dealings with Lucifer in many ways parallel those of other mediums and occultists, for example, Aleister Crowley (1875-1947) and his experiences with the 'discarnate entity' Aiwass, identified by Crowley as Satan or Lucifer. *Call Me Lucifer* will be of interest not only to readers with an interest in channeling and parapsychology, but also to students of esotericism and twentieth-century spirituality.

~ **Professor Henrik Bogdan, author of *Western Esotericism and Rituals of Initiation and co-editor of Aleister Crowley and Western Esotericism.***

"*Call me Lucifer: Dialogues with a Noble Stranger* is part of a new wave of publishing on the lives and work of leading women in the twentieth century esoteric world whose stories and roles deserve to be recognised. Irish medium Eileen J. Garrett is one such woman and her book is a fascinating account of her experiences with her most important guide and the insights for spiritual development that emerged."

~ **Vivianne Crowley, PhD, Wiccan High Priestess and author of *Wild Once: Awaken the Magic Within, and Wicca: A Comprehensive Guide to the Old Religion in the Modern World.***

"*Call Me Lucifer* is of special interest to me, having known not only Eileen Garrett but her daughter and granddaughter as well. This remarkable book resonates with the Eileen who I knew, a woman who was inquisitive, skeptical, reflective, frank, funny, and lusty. And it demonstrates how many dimensions of the human psyche are still inadequately explored, begging for answers."

~ **Stanley Krippner, Ph.D., Co-author, *Personal Mythology***

"This is a fast-paced book with surprises throughout. It should, however, be pondered as many of the book's ideas need careful contemplation. Parts of the book show theosophical influences, elsewhere hints of Gnosticism and Middle Platonism. ... Garrett is clearly a free thinker. She talks openly about her experiences of nameless sex, LSD, and distressing visions of deformed hobgoblins. Throughout all this, her charming Devil – the Noble Stranger – Lucifer. Most of the book happens in 'inner time' reminiscent of Jung's *Memories, Dreams and Reflections*. Overall, this is an interesting exploration of one woman's personal mediumship."

~ **Susan Leybourne, medium, spiritual teacher and author of** ***The Chaldean Oracles: Origins, Developments and Theurgy in Late Antiquity.***

"Psychic phenomena are matter of fact. They occur spontaneously, but perhaps only occasionally, to a large proportion of the general public. For some, psychic experiences occur so frequently that they form an essential thread of the warp and weft of lived experience. But that deep acquaintance does not necessarily lead to deep understanding of the phenomena. Eileen Garrett illustrates this perfectly. Despite a lifetime of rich spiritual experiences and an unprecedented willingness to subject herself to scientific study (a great deal of which she financed herself), she remained perplexed by their ultimate cause and wrestled with different understandings of them. Her description of interactions with 'Lucifer' – recounted here – is typically candid, as she oscillates between belief in her contact as an independent intelligent agent and belief that he has emerged from the deepest wells of her own unconscious, perhaps with a dash of extrasensory perception to account for accuracies in the information she received that couldn't be known by normal means. Communications from the Noble Stranger can be cryptic, perhaps intentionally inscrutable in the manner of a koan that is intended to be ruminated upon rather than resolved, and could reward careful study. Whatever we make of the personality that appears in these pages as 'Lucifer', and whatever we each take from his teachings, the publication of this 'lost' manuscript provides a valuable insight into the complexities of the psyche of a gifted medium."

~ **Professor Chris A. Roe, Director, Centre for Psychology & Social Sciences, University of Northampton.**

CONTENTS

FOREWORD

Eileen Jeanette Vancho Lyttle Garrett—or Eileen J. Garrett
for short—has been termed The Greatest Psychic of the
20th Century, along with a myriad of other hyperbolic
accolades. To me, first and foremost she was my much beloved
maternal grandmother, who continues to play a central role in
my life despite her passing fifty-two years ago. But her apparent
psychic functioning and her status as a very famous and well-
trusted medium have been ever-present in my family. Time and
again she astounded the world by bringing forth evidence of
the reality of her abilities—veridical information that she had
no normal ways of accessing. This was apart from her other
accomplishments as a prolific author, publisher, entrepreneur,
and founder and President of Parapsychology Foundation.

In truth, Eileen J. Garrett's so-called psychic gifts could, at
times, be more accurately considered a curse. Before I share
with you some of her biographical details, I think it best if
I first offer you an elementary explanation of the nature of
mediumistic experiences, for her and others like her, as can
be seen through history and cross-culturally.

Eileen J. Garrett was a trance medium. While in trance she
was in a state of dissociation, oblivious to her surroundings,
though somehow able to transmit and receive information

directly between herself and, apparently, consciousnesses other than her own. In the trance state, personalities referred to as "controls"—usually claiming to be a non-physical spirit or being –would communicate through her. She had several controls, and they acted as intermediaries between this world and the next. They would relay messages from other personalities in the "beyond" and communicate them to the sitter (the person who was the subject of the psychic reading). Garrett's most commonly utilized controls were two Middle Eastern gentlemen who claimed to have lived centuries ago. Uvani, the "gatekeeper," was allegedly a 13th century Arab soldier who would manifest at the beginning of a trance and ascertain what the sitter desired to learn. He would then go about trying to access this information (and possibly more) in order to meet the sitter's request. Dr. Abdul Latif, a physician, was the "psychic healer" who imparted information concerning a sitter's health, as well as spiritual insights about humankind's overall well-being.

Garrett (it seems awkward to refer to her in this rather formal manner given our loving, deeply connected relationship) was, to put it mildly, "a very strange bird." She was destined, it seemed, to be always somewhat out of the ordinary. She was born in 1893 in the Irish countryside outside of Dublin in County Meath. Her Presbyterian mother committed suicide by drowning herself three days after Eileen was born, and her Catholic Basque father took his life shortly thereafter. The infant was left in the care of her grieving and resentful maternal aunt and uncle, who already saw her mother as the family pariah, having had the poor judgment to enter into an unthinkable mixed marriage with a Catholic. And now she had the temerity to leave behind the evidence of her transgression—an orphaned daughter.

This was, in any case, the version of events that Garrett grew up believing. There is some suggestion that her aunt invented at least part of the story, perhaps to conceal an even darker truth from the young Emily Jane Savage—as Garrett was, allegedly, originally christened—or to isolate her from the rest her family. Nor is it beyond the realm of possibility that Aunt Little had psychological problems of her own and simply concocted stories for her vulnerable young niece. Garrett may actually have been born in 1892, a year earlier than she believed; her mother's drowning may have been precipitated by an epileptic seizure; and her father may have been an entirely different person than she thought[1]. Like much of Garrett's life, these details remain shrouded in mystery. But whatever the case, her early beginnings were anything but auspicious and both accounts point to a traumatic, turbulent childhood. Added to these events, Garrett was soon ostracized as she revealed her psychic gifts, which alarmed and frightened the locals. Referred to as the "Devil's Spawn" and tormented by all when she talked about her strange experiences or related information communicated to her from beyond, she escaped to London at the age of fifteen. She achieved this through an impromptu marriage, specifically in hopes of leaving behind her sad beginnings—and her psychic functioning.

This, however, was not to be. Her mediumistic abilities grew ever more present in her life, and in fact became a major factor in the termination of two of her three marriages. The other husband was killed in battle during the First World War, an event which Garrett had predicted, then horribly envisioned at the moment of his death. More heartache came with the loss of three sons, and the near-loss of her only daughter, my mother.

By 1922, it had become clear to Garrett that the spirit voices and experiences could no longer be ignored, and she placed herself in the hands of James Hewat McKenzie of the British College of Psychic Science. McKenzie was instrumental in helping her come to grips with her psychic gifts—training and disciplining her mediumship so she could function productively both within and beyond the psychic world, and preventing it from intruding upon her private life. She was relieved to discover that she was not losing her mind after all, as she had

---

[1]   See Healey, Joan (1986) Letter in *Journal of the Society for Psychical Research*, 54: 806, pp. 90–92

long feared. Nevertheless, she continued throughout her entire life to question the source of her psychic abilities, as well as how and why she had been "chosen" to have them. Years of working as a trance medium and honing her other psychic modalities ensued. This prompted her first visit to the United States in 1931, when she was brought to New York by the American Society for Psychical Research (ASPR) for testing in scientific investigations of psychic phenomena. This was the start of a lifetime of willing and even eager volunteering of her services for research. She traveled to California in 1932 and met many of nascent Hollywood's movers and shakers, including Cecil B. de Mille who was so impressed with her psychic gifts and messages from his dead mother that, until his death, whenever Garrett was in town her room was filled with flowers from the grateful producer. During World War II, while staying with her French lover in the Côte d'Azur, she ran a soup kitchen at an orphanage for the French resistance. She became trapped by the German advance, however, and had to flee over the mountains to Portugal. There she pawned her fur coat to buy a ticket on one of the last tramp steamers out of Lisbon, bound for New York.

Garrett then embarked on various business enterprises as the world of commerce always intrigued her. Indeed, her career accomplishments alone set her apart from most women of her day, lying outside the social mores of the times. From her early days until her death, she was a magnet for all sorts of interesting and creative individuals. In the 1940s she founded Creative Age Press and became a "lady publisher," something seen as extraordinary in those times. She mixed with the crème de la crème of New York literary circles, and rubbed shoulders with luminaries in theater, art, and politics. Her publishing parties were legend, and in fact she was told by Patrick Dennis that she was one of the inspirations for his most famous character, the eponymous *Auntie Mame*. Her collection of friends ranged from Tallulah Bankhead to Aldous Huxley, from Anaïs Nin and Robert Graves to Bill Wilson, the founder of Alcoholics

Anonymous, to mention just a few. Her academic friends included the prominent and influential Swiss psychiatrists Adolf Meyer and C. G. Jung.

She never completely left the publishing field, authoring four novels under the *nom de plume* Jean Lyttle, and, more importantly, several books on mediumship. These included three separate autobiographies in which she sought answers to lifelong questions raised by her psychic functioning, written for the benefit of both herself and the field of psychical research—and indeed, for all of humankind. These books show a deep and serious dedication to facing and disentangling the complexities of her life and especially to understanding her mediumship from both scientific and spiritual perspectives. The first, *My Life as a Search for the Meaning of Mediumship*, was published in 1939, and will soon be back in print from Afterworlds Press. The second, *Adventures in the Supernormal: A Personal Memoir* (1949) is available in a recent edition from the Parapsychology Foundation website[2] (where you will also find a wealth of information about Garrett's gifts and accomplishments).

Both the source of her controls and the meaning of her gifts were perpetual mysteries to Garrett, as reflected in Part I of this book. Always a critical thinker—even when it came to her own lived experience—Garrett was not at all sure that she was actually in communication with the dead. She believed that it was possible that the phenomena she experienced were merely functions of telepathy, and that she might be picking up information from the sitters themselves in this life rather than dead souls residing in the Great Beyond. I have always wondered why the telepathy interpretation would be any more or less extraordinary than the possibility of her mediumship being evidence for survival after death.

Though no longer working professionally as a medium, Garrett continued to volunteer her services for research around the world, hoping only to push forward human understanding

---

[2]   www.parapsychology.org

of the riddles presented by parapsychology. To that end, in 1951 she co-founded the non-profit Parapsychology Foundation. With the generosity of her long-time friend, the Honorable Frances P. Bolton, Congresswoman of Ohio, she fulfilled her vision of a worldwide forum supporting scientific exploration of psychic phenomena. For over seventy years, the Foundation has funded research, supported publishing and conference programs, and housed a library for psychical researchers. Eileen J. Garrett died September 15, 1970, still on her quest for better understanding of the mysteries of the psychic world that preoccupied so much of her life.

Let me now share with you how the materials in the present book came to light. Upon Garrett's death, she left in the care of my mother and myself a number of "Mystery Boxes." For years during her work on the Parapsychology Foundation, Garrett pushed the details of her own lifetime of mediumship to the back burner. She literally packed away in file boxes all her papers related to it, fearing that it could impede the progress of the science of parapsychology. She knew she had a difficult road to walk, and that even as researchers applied scientific methodology to the study of these complex phenomena, the field was also rife with fraud and opportunism. This is reflected in her comment, "If the whole, strange, mystifying psychic gift could be snatched out of the darkness of séance rooms and put into the capable probing hands of science, everybody would feel much better about the subject and the world of science and philosophy could be enriched." Another statement illustrative of her ambivalence and frustration in working with psychic matters: "On Monday, Wednesday, Friday I believe in the paranormal and on Tuesday, Thursday, and Saturday, I don't. And on Sunday I don't give a damn!" I have come to realize that was not truly the case—of course, she *did* ultimately give a damn as I fully appreciate when opening and reading the contents of her Mystery Boxes.

As is the case with most philanthropic organizations (and especially those dedicated to psychical research), these are desperate financial times. With resources for the Parapsychology Foundation practically non-existent, I have turned to these boxes covered in decades of dust, searching for previously unknown, unpublished gems in hopes that their publication might help to raise funds that will enable the Foundation to continue our valuable work. This amazing cache of material is valuable not only for the history and progress of the field, but, I am convinced, is also of great and lasting value to humankind. On a personal level, it also gives me a greater understanding of a woman I so loved and admired.

As a teen, I was aware of Garrett's conversations with an entity she referred to as the Noble Stranger, whom she encountered intermittently throughout her lifetime. His existence was rarely spoken of outside the family and a very small circle of Garrett's intimate friends. She described him as a sophisticated, attractive, but rather cold figure.

As I matured I would be pressed into stenographic duties, transcribing and typing her handwritten experiences and conversations with this figure, often immediately following his visitations. My mother, Eileen Coly, the Parapsychology Foundation's second President, faithfully preserved these papers, adding them to the Mystery Boxes along with other transcriptions of trance sittings, correspondence, and interviews (with Garrett as herself and Garrett entranced by her controls). All these heretofore lost introspections and channeled treatises have enabled me to form a more complete characterization of my grandmother.

When I first read through this collection of Noble Stranger material, I was surprised to learn that only when urged by Dr. Nandor Fodor, the psychoanalyst, famed psychical researcher, and long-time colleague and friend of Garrett, did she finally ask her Noble Stranger his name. The response she "received" was astonishing: "You may call me Lucifer."

I was puzzled, to say the least, as to why she never divulged to me the fact that the Noble Stranger she was in apparent conversation with was, allegedly, none other than *Lucifer*! At a later date, however, the Mystery Boxes yielded the answer to me. I discovered an old a carbon copy of a portion of a letter in which Garrett wrote that she did not want to talk about "Lucifer" because she already had enough trouble in her mediumistic life—particularly skepticism about the very concept of her controls speaking through her—without bringing *him* into the mix! In hindsight, she was probably correct.

The fact that she kept such detailed and meticulous records of her experiences with him, however, underscores his importance to her life. Much of the material sprang from questions posed to Lucifer by Dr. Emilio Servadio, one of Italy's leading psychoanalysts, and includes Lucifer's lucid responses. The rest stems from interviews with Garrett in trance, mostly in the Spring of 1958; and from her personal journals.

In the first part of this book, Garrett describes her initial encounters with Lucifer, traces her history with him, and recounts their numerous conversations. Characteristically, she also interrogates her own reactions to the encounters, delving into her own psychology in relation to them, and even questions the nature of the Noble Stranger's existence—or nonexistence. As indicated by references to the 1969 moon landing, this part of the book was completed towards the end of Garrett's life, though it incorporates earlier material. How long she worked on the manuscript, and for what purpose, remain unknown.

Yet another mystery surrounding Lucifer may be found in interviews between the American depth psychologist Ira Progoff and Garrett's first control, Uvani. With Garrett under trance, Progoff asked Uvani for more information about Lucifer, who would come to Garrett "while she is awake, while she walks by the sea ... who stands beside her, over her shoulder, or in front of her." He is one "with whom she argues, and who argues with her," and "who speaks with her about her confusions" as Progoff portrayed it. In response, Uvani communicated through Garrett that Lucifer was, in fact, one and the same as Tahoteh—yet another control, from the ancient pagan world. Uvani described Tahoteh as "a great teacher, a great life keeper," and "the giver of signs and words," a being of great power who "has walked among men for many eons." He added somewhat ominously, "I hope she treats him with respect." Progoff concluded that Lucifer was "another psychic representation of the Tahoteh figure"[3]—though that gets us no closer to a real understanding of the nature of these entities.

An additional dynamic continues to puzzle me greatly. In the Mystery Boxes, within two different séance transcripts, the control Abdul Latif "communicated" that he had saved my mother from death when she was a child. He did this, he explained, not for her own sake or for the sake of Garrett, but for the sake of the soul that was to come ... the daughter's daughter, "The One Who Comes After." You can perhaps imagine, therefore, the pressure I feel as I scramble to understand what my role could be—if in fact it can be believed that I indeed have one (like my grandmother, I walk the narrow path between belief and disbelief).

At first it seemed plausible to me that I was supposed to share with the public Garrett's conversations with her Noble Stranger. Of the opinion that I should not be the only one privy to the contents of these documents, I submitted Garrett's writings to the publisher, confident that I was acting as a good steward of my grandmother's legacy. But in a wave of skepticism I became filled with misgivings and was concerned that the manuscript might be considered a mere oddity. With growing anxiety, while in the process of inventorying Garrett's papers I turned at random to yet another dormant Mystery Box. And

---

[3] Progoff, Ira (1964) *The Image of an Oracle: A Report on Research into the Mediumship of Eileen J. Garrett.* New York: Helix Press, pp. 26-28, 40.

voila! As if in answer to a plea, I put my hands directly on additional commentary from Lucifer that neither my mother nor I knew existed—fully prepared and ready for publication. This document forms the second part of this book, Lucifer's Compendium of Guidance. Perhaps there is a plan, and I have fulfilled my role after all.

Thus, as the current President of the Parapsychology Foundation (following my grandmother and mother in matrilineal succession), I am proud to be able finally to bring this book to light—newly discovered and available for the first time, for your consideration and conjecture. You will no doubt draw your own conclusions as to its value, as I must draw my own, though I will say that much of the material seems to speak directly to me as I suspect it may also speak to you. I believe it may aid in our greater understanding of the self, and perhaps even the meaning of life. The first part of this book—just before Lucifer's Compendium of Guidance—ends with Garrett's somewhat dire warning and clarion call for mankind to take heed of Lucifer's commentary in hopes of saving ourselves in more ways than one.

Eileen Garrett died in her beloved South of France, presumably stilling the voice of her Noble Stranger. Of course, one wonders if perhaps he is *somewhere*, presently engaged in dialogue with other chosen souls. In any event, I trust that Lucifer will be happy with our interest in his words, and should he think to appear once again, I for one would be most happy to make his acquaintance.

Lisette Coly
New York City
June 2022

BOOK ONE

CALL ME LUCIFER

A Companion of Sorts

I have put to myself for more than half a century the same question: What produces seeming hallucinations, spontaneously and without introspection, from the deep subconscious areas of the self in me and others experiencing psychic phenomena? I have worked continually within the field of psychical research and have been trained for ten years to produce evidence that would appear to answer spontaneously, in and out of a trance state, questions that are concerned with the spectral images of the dead and whether they exist in an afterlife.

I am too close to the phenomena I produce to be able to analyze the results objectively. The fantasy of the inner seeing, hearing and knowing is second nature to me and I have had to accept it since the kind of evidence that it produces relates itself to those who have come to me through the years to seek advice. I have been therefore the "puppet" which produces evidence that has sustained many people through deep loss. The "I" is not visible, but the "it" takes over and produces the drama known as extra sensory perception.

Many individuals have these gifts to some degree—they can pursue several trains of thought and find comprehensive answers. My alleged controls, there are two, gather the millions of assembled thoughts from the alleged dead to give comfort to the living. I have spent long years suggesting to myself that I am a good mind reader; but that is not enough, for the minds of *others* are too often involved in the phases of what is termed communication.

I have written about this problem in previous books[4], but there is another aspect of this mental activity that concerns me and has continued to do so since 1936. I have a companion of sorts who arrives spontaneously at times chosen by him and, I surmise, excites the cervical nervous system to enable means and ways by which he enters into a dialogue with me.

---

[4] Most notably in My Life as a *Search for the Meaning of Mediumship* (1939: Afterworlds Press reprint 2022).

Spawn of the Devil

I believe it all came about in my early years, when I first went to school. My imagination was thought to be respondent to something that my teachers, family and others referred to as my being, in my own person, "the Spawn of the Devil." I heard this term repeated by my elders so often that I finally found myself able to detach a part of me and send it long or short distances to absorb information that could and did answer meaningful questions for those bereaved. Clearly, the mind is at rest until the enquirer arrives who will sit quietly and await the answer to his questions, not apparent until I enter the trance state—a facility I use as the priest may enter into solitude to hear the confession of some unknown citizen who has sought him out to be helped.

I have watched myself at work and know rather well how devoid I can be of any measure of knowledge that will reveal itself when the enquirer enters my presence. Then, spontaneously, the magic works and some part of my own mind receives the answer that will remove the anxiety of those who came to enquire. I can produce at will answers to the questions of the bereaved—or do I become in that moment a machine capable of entering into the mind of the enquirer to bring forth answers that will allay the grief and anxieties of those who seek my services, keeping them adjusted when a partner has given up life or a beloved relation or parent is no more? How do I know that I will find answers? I know because for more than half a century I have been doing this service willingly and gladly.

And He Disappeared

When I first heard myself described as "Spawn of the Devil" I was sincerely afraid, for the dogma of the Roman Catholic Church must have given food for thought to my subconscious mind. I dreamt on several occasions that I was being pursued by Satan. In fact, I grew fearful of the moment that announced bedtime. The Priest was called to deal with my fears and phantasms, which continued for the duration of my adolescent existence.

Then, in 1936, standing outside of Harrods Department Store in Kensington, London, I became aware of a man who caused my heart to beat wildly. I was unable to walk away. I believe to this day that he approached me with an air of a school master and advised me that introspection in front of a store of this nature produced temptation to spend monies that would be better employed in acquiring knowledge, more helpful to my nature than looking at various things within the shop far beyond my economic reach. Instead, this figure seriously advised that my spare hours of recreation would be better employed by visiting the Museum of Natural History nearby. I found myself at the door of the museum—and he disappeared.

Someone Like the Sun and the Stars

In hindsight, my first introduction to this "Noble Stranger" must have been between the ages of three and four, with dream experiences of a particularly nightmarish quality. My aunt discovered me on many occasions crying in my sleep and breathing very heavily, which may have been brought about by the fact that, when I first went to school, I was the only Protestant child among Catholics and, therefore, came in for a great deal of persecution. I was even bedeviled by the other children, sometimes beaten up if I protested to my teachers; but always I was told that as a Protestant I must go to Hell. Hell was a meaningless word to me and still remains so. But the devil process must have entered into these conversations, because for all my years I have remembered being called "Spawn of the Devil."

For those who have not been brought up in the self-centered Roman Catholic religion, it would seem improbable that one would have such a great difficulty at such an early age; but historically it has been related again and again that the trouble between Protestant and Catholic remains, through time, viciously alive within the Emerald Island.

At home, I heard a good deal about the need to live rightly and justly, so that Jehovah, God of Battles, would look kindly upon us. My aunt was too taken up with her devotions in her Presbyterian Church to understand very much what was happening to the heart of a child. My uncle, who had spent the better part of his life in India, did on occasion approach the school community and spoke rather sharply to the teachers concerning my plight. I then gritted my teeth and made the conclusion in my own mind that if my schoolmates continued to make life so very difficult, then I would have to become aggressive and hit back. Finally, through all my National School days, I did win my battles and became the ringleader of all that was mischievous, earning the reputation for myself that I was not to be taken too lightly.

I left the school with honors at the age of ten. By this time, I consciously thought very little about the devil. I remembered, however, a great deal about my dreams and fancies picturing him as tall, vital and strong. I had always been told by my presumably imaginary playmates, "the children," that he was very red, and this produced in me a curious reaction. From my earliest days I became very attached to that color and wherever I went I took a piece of red calico, muslin, or any other material of that vibrant color; it became a kind of fetish. This fetish of mine was easily kept amongst my schoolbooks or in my workbasket or about my person. In one way or another I held on to it. Even to this day I am most happy when I have had a red handkerchief to which I can cling.

I kept the image of the devil in my mind during the whole of my adolescence, mainly because one heard continually the old superstitions and legends, which surround him. In my adolescent years, I believe he became mixed up with an image of Brian Boru, a Danish giant who was supposed to have walked in seven-league boots[5]. Legend and history can get mixed up in the minds of local people, and it must be said of them who work the soil that they are very superstitious.

After I left the National School, I spent a small period of time at home where I could give way to my Devil fantasy, both in my waking state and in my dream experiences. Whenever things went wrong in my childish world, it was toward this invisible figure that I turned and invariably, while I kept to myself, I regarded him as one of my friends.

Once, in walking through the beautiful green fields, I looked up quickly and saw a very handsome stranger—stranger because I knew most of the people around. Though he was tall and gave one a sense of inner awe, he gave me the impression of vitality being within, and finally I accepted his presence without questioning it. Thus began my waking experiences of the "Noble Stranger" and I came to the conclusion that I had someone who was able to look after me; someone like the sun and the stars that was there in any emergency. As I looked at him very straight in the face and asked him: "Who are you? Where have you come from?" he returned my stare somewhat quizzically and disappeared.

Woe Betide You

From the age, therefore, of three or four years, until I was nineteen, I had this invisible friend with whom I could hold conversations and who, in his own way, made life rather easy for me. I was able to ask him about the meaning of sin, a word that was often on the lips of my friends. I was also troubled because I was told by my aunt that I had no faith. With mature introspection over the years, I realize that I had gone through

---

[5]   According to the folklore of various European countries, seven-league boots enabled the wearer to stride many kilometers in one step.

my marriages and prevailed, and made good, but that this had little to do with the long hours I'd spent reading the Bible as a child, which I was forced to do as punishment. I knew by heart the five books, from Genesis to Deuteronomy, but even so, looking back, I realize now that the more I read and re-read them, the more puzzled I became. My aunt's emphasis on the old, jealous, domineering, non-merciful god caused me to spend a good deal of time in preoccupation.

Of my own accord, after the loss of two of my children I turned to the New Testament, looking for something that would give me the faith to carry on. The pages of the New Testament seemed just as obscure and, at times, unreasonable.

Finally, I made up my mind that the God of Israel was a tribal god and that I was only in contact with one part of the religion, but that other people in different parts of the world must be guided by different interpretations as to the destiny of man. I began to think in terms of other philosophies such as that of Islam, and even turned to Chinese philosophy, escaping the rather tiresome attitude, which appears to evolve through the Bible as one reads about that impertinent God of Israel.

It is only fair to say that I was in revolt against Him; and this served me also through the years to be in revolt against any form of dictatorship—not only the dictators themselves but also those who serve them. The tragedy of the Passion, those simple fishermen who followed the Son of God, the carpenter's son and his crucifixion became as real to me as did the Greek dramas. As I grew older I could not accept Christianity as my relations and friends accepted it.

When I lost my sons to meningitis and turned to the Rector of my church and allowed him to know a little of my inner thinking, he warned: "Woe betide you; you are fast falling into the hands of the devil!"

Noble Stranger

In time, I began to receive the visits of he whom I thought of as the "Noble Stranger" in much the same way as I accepted the existence of my control personalities Uvani and Dr. Abdul Latif. Through the years I have given much thought to the meaning of the symbol of the man who comes and goes and leaves me unable to solve his reasons to my own satisfaction. I can dispose momentarily of the existence of the control personalities that rule my life by explaining them away as being discovered perhaps in my fantasy journeys, or as names from literature or deeply buried in the subconscious, but I have a great difficulty in comprehending the meaning of his visits. I encountered him once in England's Devil's Dyke, and I continue to meet him in dreams as well as what appears to be "in the flesh."

The late Dr. Nandor Fodor was interested in the appearance of this one that had become, in a sense, like a lost brother. Under hypnosis he vaguely connected the "Noble Stranger" as being related to my first hypnotist. But it was only Uvani, my first control personality, that was in any way connected with Mr. Huhnli who first put me into a deep hypnotic sleep. It was Dr. Fodor who suggested that I ask my visitor his name. To myself, I always called him the "Noble Stranger", and then one day I did ask him: "What may I call you? You have come to see me often enough and I think it is time that you really introduced yourself".

His answer was: "You can call me Lucifer." I was shocked.

Neither Good Nor Evil

I do not think I had any real feeling for what the devil might be like. I have never been able to accept a Heaven on the other side of space, neither could I at any time in my life believe that there was a Hell into which some of us would be demoted. Since we are all in a state of imperfection, who is there amongst us to make the division between the good and not so good? And certainly Lucifer, as he said I may call him, gave me a sense of awe but not of fear.

He has a strictness in presenting ideas that I found intriguing. I have asked him: "Is it true that you cause conflict in the lives of men?" and he said: "No, not exactly. It is part of man's inheritance to grow through repeated mistakes and suffering. Ignorance of the law has also narrowed the moral codes of mankind."

When I asked him if he associated himself with any particular doctrine, he was sardonic and replied: "Certainly not. Man himself has made his own ideal to take upon himself the power and glory to decide what is righteous and what is good. All dogmas, from the beginning of time, have grown from man's own fear of the kingdom, which he is permitted to inherit. These dogmas speak of love but they rarely contain anything that is truly charitable."

His speeches are curiously and beautifully molded. There is neither good nor evil in his pronouncements; nor does he seek to make clear that good and evil are opposites. He admits of many aspects to his nature: conflict and dualism being parts of it. He remarks that he best serves those who speak so sternly of the moral codes. "Be certain," he emphasizes, "that the codes are not for themselves, but for others."

He rarely speaks of love as such, but remarks that man is inherently on a long journey which goes far beyond his present life span; that the substance of his mind and will must be tempted many times, so it is useless, he says, to speak of good and evil as though they were opposites. "What is good for one may not be so good for one's neighbor. Man is better off by living from within and finding his own way without rites, invocations, or the need for power. If man says that this is not so, it stems from the hypocrisy which is deep in the nature of man's thinking.

"When these aspects arise and man enters into them, you know very well that he has departed from the center of himself and has now got up in what is called doing good in politics, religion, etc., in the name of some god or master; and when he does this, he naturally beclouds his own deep unconscious knowledge that he has departed from simplicity."

These are strong words, and I have many times dismissed him as a literary fantasy, a device perhaps presented by the subconscious, necessary to him so that I can communicate with him on levels where words do not seem to matter. If he has undue influence over me—as it has been suggested—I do not detect it. Others might find some of his remarks cynical, even diabolic. Cold and ruthless he is at times, but when he departs one feels that one has been put through a severe examination of oneself.

During my life I have read much on the subject relating to the devil, and when I told him this I asked him who created him, to which he replied: "Each man has to have a symbol upon which he can hang his weakness. Remember, in your early days when you read of the parents of the world, Adam and Eve. When they had allegedly sinned—as the patriarchs wrote at that time—man was the weaker of the two and said 'The woman tempted me and I did eat.'

"Wizards have always been spoken of from earliest times. Man cannot hope to reach the godhead but he is happy and content with something less, and, throughout history, necromancy has had a definite place. And women, too, are witches at heart."

I asked after this statement: "Do you claim any particular group to have given you to the world?"

To which he replied: "If you mean the Jewish or Christian, Assyrian, Roman or Etruscan, the answer is no. Each generation has need of me. The act of getting into contact with a great vital force is not part of man's heritage yet."

I asked him at this point: "Do you appear in the days when men were unable to use the written word?"

He said: "Long before, for man had always hieroglyphics by which to confuse their enemies. The appearance of the artistic or written word are the hieroglyphs which man used for centuries. They were, of themselves, arts which concealed the true meaning from the untutored; but it was in the days when man was more simple and the priests made the theater which gave man the sense of being in contact with something better than himself."

"Were the priests always truthful?" I asked.

To which he replied: "Seldom. In the dark ages or what is called your civilized culture of today which, by its very sophistication, is entirely corrupt."

He denies lightly the conception of angelic beings falling from another form of existence to live in alien captivity. When I have questioned him closely he adds that the appearance of the written word was more ingeniously a part of human corruption than the art that preceded it, which concealed its true meaning from the untutored.

He will not agree that his coming was announced because of the strict moral gates between man and woman, but he says that there never has been a time when man desired union with the vital and the absolute.

There is no art of necromancy. I have over the years dismissed that as a literary fantasy. I have been alert for undue influence, to be certain that my "Stranger" was not putting things into my mind without my knowledge. I do not think so. I regard him with great interest; his ruthlessness is hard to take at times but, finally, one realizes it is not devoid of truth.

I have read a great deal that concerns itself with aspects of the "Noble Stranger" as I prefer to call him. It is difficult to place him in any particular climate. He has no relationship to our present-day Hebrew or Christian inheritance, nor does he speak of the Romans or the Etruscans. He does not accept the fact that he was "sent" with the arrival and growth of knowledge between man and woman, but intimates the existence of a divine supernatural abroad in the world of man, against which man himself sets himself. He admits, however, of his own union with the final and the absolute.

When I ask him if there is a state within man from which a complete purity can spring, he answers that these inheritors are there to win through by faith. I have asked if divine power is stronger than his own. He answered: "Yes, but my power does not derive from the dogma devised by man."

When he arrives, he displays an air of tolerance—neither belief nor disbelief in any of the questions I raise. Whenever he visits me I have a number of questions, which he receives sometimes with solemnity, and sometimes with ironic laughter. He tells me "evolution in allness is the process, ever changingness." As far as I can understand he is principle—perhaps "one's own still small voice" seeking in the wilderness for meaning that permits one to use responsibility as a sacred device. He informs me that "Man is the instigator of his own revelations and sets about changing these revelations as the times and customs demand change."

The World is My Theater

I have questioned him about the various disguises that he is alleged to use to cover himself. What of the Greek attire I once saw him in, the mask and the headdress? And what of the tail and claw—which I have never come into contact with myself—but which he is alleged to use? He tells me rather casually that he can wear garb that makes it easy for him to make his presence felt. "Think nothing of it," he said; "the world is my theater in which I play my roles." I have asked him repeatedly, was he more than this? He answers "More, much more and even less."

I inquire about the rituals, the covens with special foods, delicious and delicate, served with obscenity. "Yes, yes all that." One of his more thoughtful and sober statements is: "Man conceived it all, and eats of it until the full consciousness of decay takes over. This consciousness is always abroad, to take over alike the community and the solitary. Man will pursue his malefic art and demand an accomplice as long as the planet lasts."

He speaks of "two schools forever busy; those who reject evil with sternness to cause untold unhappiness, and those who neglect it altogether, to be overcome by it."

"From this generous world there are always formidable doctrines taking over to impinge and swallow the rest," he once told me, "Man will reflect my image, but, you see, I have to be imagined in order to be rejected."

I once asked him: "Are you lonely in your self-appointed task?"

And he said: "No, there is no need for loneliness as long as the planet lasts," which I thought at the time was a thoughtful and sober statement. "Man gives me many images", he told me, "and I have to fit into each one so that I be not rejected."

Every Grain of Sand

What still remains to be answered is by what means have I created this being? I am, as I know myself, not given to invocation; unless mediumship itself is a form of invocation, or demand and desire, but this I use sparingly and for the greater good. I regard prayer as a deep desire to help and to aid those who are in need. Where then does this "Noble Stranger" arrive from? By what means of thought does he appear to spontaneously discuss the nature of man? Perhaps I conceived of these devil interludes and I am arguing with the process of evolution of my own being, which he seems to represent?

Dr. Emilio Servadio, the famed Italian psychoanalyst, once asked me if I thought that the "Noble Stranger" gives me answers that are in a large sense unexpected. I have to say honestly "No." I think that he draws out unexplained dimensions in my own thoughtfulness, thoughts of human nature, and, of course, of myself, because everything boils down finally to my own place within the cosmos.

Our encounters have been in the nature of dialogue: rather like working on the composition of a novel, but there have been no plans. These "conversations" appear to take place when I am ill, frustrated, or in need of another point of view.

His usefulness when I have dialogues with him is that he generally speaks of human nature as a whole. One of his remarks, with which I resonate, is that "every grain of sand is important; therefore, every human being has his work to do and lives out, sometimes in a reflective sense, the deep meaning of his life as he sees it." He does drain my thoughts away from the everyday methods of living and from the life of nature around me; and this is equally important to him as the way of man himself. I agree that every grain of sand is important, and then I ask myself why is every grain of sand important? Why is every leaf important? And such reflections give me a very much deeper sense toward the day than I would have had myself. I set out with one set of emotions and ideas, and by the time I have allowed his remarks to sink in, it becomes an accelerating experience; it turns my thoughts to the evolution of the life of the tree, of the plant, of the animal, until I see in perspective many things of extreme importance.

There are various aspects of feelings towards him that occur during our dialogues. I have been asked if he gives me a vague feeling of sadness or elation, or do I experience a typical emotional state similar to which you might feel for somebody whom you respect and love?

I would say that I am in a deeply emotional state when we converse; but it is not in any way connected with the emotion of love, but rather of awe. Remember that he sometimes scolds me, but this, too, is in keeping with the early pattern of my life, when I appeared to bring down the wrath of my aunt on my head, and after the hurt was over, I realized her point of view.

In the same way, I come away from our dialogues excited. I do not feel any sadness when the dialogue finishes; I am inclined to think that I have spent a long time daydreaming and yet it cannot be described as such for in my life there is no time for daydreaming. Of course, his presence leaves me to face myself in a thousand different ways. I have to regard the world's actions, and he warns me of the mistakes that we make continually as a people and a nation. When I consider these conditions and truly understand them, I feel sad—mostly because these are things I can do nothing about.

I feel after his visit that all things are starkly clear, and that it has been so with yesterday's ten thousand years. That gives me a feeling of elation and I feel, in a sense, purged and purified. I may thereafter be sad for hours, with a great sense of impotence which makes me continually ask myself: "Will I ever comprehend the true meaning of life?"

His personality is that of a man who has seen so much and known so much that he appears to be tired of the stupidity of mankind who undoubtedly will leave in its wake nothing but destruction; for every new aspect which can be called progress leaves behind it the loss of tranquility. When he points out the mistakes that have been made by man's wanton greed, evident through my own lifetime, I have to agree with him that for all the good that has come of so-called progress, man does very little to clean up the world which he is fast destroying. It is not only that man himself pushes his simpler brother out of the way, but also that he pollutes the atmosphere both on land and in water.

Recently, I talked to him about man's desire to reach the moon. He tells me: "Well, that was a piece of your planet at one time which, because of its many volcanic eruptions has laid waste to life. But when man arrives there with his tools, he is bound to leave behind him the germs of his own make up and so, life on the moon can never be the same again."

I take this as another proof of man's failure. "Will we people the moon?" I ask.

"If so," he replied, "you would only make trouble for yourselves. Every place that man has gone, he has brought with him the means and ways to make progress possible—but the progression has been with guns and with a deep desire to possess. Look back into History as far as you will and try to imagine, as you must, what a beautiful planet the earth was, and now it is doomed to be destroyed—not in your lifetime, I hope—but it is obvious that man, in the name of progress, does take away from the simplicity of living. Man is now not content with the disaster, which he refuses to look at—he now wants to reach the planets, and for no good reason.

"When you stop to look around, you see that whatever part of me is in man—and you suggest that there is a part because I have come through every process of evolution—you tell me I must be involved in it."

This leaves me depressed, with a cosmic sadness. I realize that we have everything here and now with which we could do great good, and I think of myself in relation to everything that breathes. It must be true, for you see that even the jungles in Vietnam are no more, and we fight a bitter war, obviously to kill since we cannot hope to win. And if we should win, as has happened in Japan, we leave resentments that the years cannot wipe out.

I remember once saying to him: "Oh, it cannot be as bad as you say."

To which he replied in an offhand manner: "When the American Civil War occurred between North and South, was there any real need for it and have things in general improved?"

He often leaves me in the midst of a conflict like this. Yet he is stimulating—in a sense heroic. He sees through us and finally, it must be true that he presents the easier way which, of course, is not always the way to good.

A Divinity of Wrongdoing

I rebel against some of the things that he tells me, very definitely. On the other hand, I think that I anticipate his "scolding." It is in keeping with the pattern of my life that I do bring down upon my head some things. Sometimes I get very cross. I think I may have just dreamt it all. It is like daydreaming, but, on the other hand, it isn't really, because it does make me think deeply.

I have to face up to myself in a thousand different ways; I have to face up to the world's illness. The most terrible realization is the foreknowledge that his discussions give me, of the terrible mistakes that we make continually—as a people and a nation. When the slate has been cleaned, I can start all over again. I have a similar sentiment as I go about my day of "being good." Each day before I leave my office, I want to know if all is in order, because if my "slate is clean" I feel confident in a day well lived.

When I get a stiff talking-to from the entity who somehow emerges as the "Noble Stranger," I sometimes feel very sad, and sometimes very tired, with a sense of "Oh heavens, when will I ever understand the meaning of life, or the meaning of myself?" He leaves me in his wake with a terrific feeling of resignation, but also a feeling that I must keep myself well and on an even keel, as one cannot abandon life even if you know it is going to turn out badly. Perhaps this explains my ongoing motivation to leave nothing unresolved, or as I say, to attempt continually to "keep the slate clean" even though there is the realization that nothing good is intended to come out of the effort. This is what is so disheartening.

I remain wide-eyed asking: "Oh, when can it be different?"

He just touches on this occasionally and says: "But you see, there is no intention of making it different," and laughs over it and adds: "Well, my work goes on. It does not lessen."

In a way, he is a kind of—what shall we say—divinity of wrongdoing. He not only expects it, but also tells *you* what to expect—it is going to go this way or that. Then I ask myself and him: "What is the use of thus doing anything?"

He says: "Ah, but for you, of course," looking at me with a rather sardonic expression, "For you, of course, each day has to be just a little better, doesn't it?"

I quickly responded, "Well for you too! You once told me that when we fall from grace you suffer. What about that?"

He admits: "This is true."

The odd part of it is that, although he dooms everything to failure, and one sees it very clearly, I personally don't agree with this at all because, no matter how many times my own plans come apart, he has also taught me that just because they do fall apart, one must never give up. You have to try and try again, very often. He reminds me: "When you were a little child, you know, you have no idea how many times you had fallen down and hurt yourself very badly, but each time you picked yourself up. And so, man must do it." He is aware of weakness and elated by it.

Every Process of Evolution

I have been asked if there is any correlation between these apparitions and a particular hour of the day, the seasons or weather conditions. Weather does play a very important role in my life. I am aware of every change in temperature. I sense rain in the air; I smell the changes in the wind; I watch the moon and the stars for storm and good weather.

When I have to do anything in the telepathic area, I do it by throwing myself into what I have learned to regard as the pool of memory for answers. I have the means of exploring in this area, and very naturally, being so very much aware of the elements as I am, they have a great deal to do with my state of mind, my state of wellbeing.

I can't imagine looking for him on a dull day. My spirits have to be really "bright." I have to be in a good mood, in a searching mood, as I am much more curious on a very bright moonlit or starry night, or on a very clear and exciting day. I don't ever seek him in a depressed mood or in depressing weather.

It has been said that there is the image of an oracle and the image of an executive dynatype contained in me[6]. The Oracle plans and preconceives and precognizes the development of events, but then in their actual administration, obstacles in life

---

[6] See Ira Progoff (1964) *The Image of an Oracle: A Report on Research into the Mediumship of Eileen J. Garrett.* New York: Helix Press.

arise. I question myself as to whether I create a sort of conflict in which I then turn to "the Noble Stranger" and confront him saying "Look what has just happened!"

I do see things happening, sometimes weeks or months ahead, but that does not trouble me in the least. I know that a set of circumstances is traveling towards me, but I do not want to know when it will arrive. In my administrative work, providing a thing is set up and arranged, I am not in the least interested to continually discuss or dwell on it. If a piece of work has to be done, I want it to be well done; but if nothing comes from it, I am not overly disappointed. I am not too upset when aspects have not turned out as I would have them.

My whole preoccupation with my "Noble Stranger" is on an entirely different level. I am looking for the answers to my own inabilities to deal with myself in relation to the whole of life.

I am able to see the plans of men clearly, each one preying on everyone else. I am not responsible for it, but there is a part of me that is resigned to accept it. He remarks: "Because you have come through every process of evolution, so you are involved in it."

I do not consciously search for him. I encounter him when I want questions answered, not about myself as a person, but myself in relation to the palm tree or the flow of life around— myself in relation to the table that "breathes" and would like to vanish because it is old and has served its time. Myself in relation to old things in the house that reveal their story and would like to cease to be held in "imprisonment." Myself in relation to the scene, to the time that the jungle will be no more; then he may suddenly appear in the jungle and I tell him: "Leave this for a few more years so that this jungle will continue to thrive."

He replies: "No, certainly not. It has no true foundation."

Then we get into a really significant harangue, which is very stimulating. I finally declare: "Well, you are not omnipotent. You just have so much more knowledge than I can conceive! It is exhilarating to have an argument with you!"

After he leaves me following such a "conversation" I know I can't win my argument. I know he is essentially correct, because invariably when I pick up my newspaper the next morning I can again hear his sardonic laugh while I read of more complexities and conflicts between nations! He sees through us all! He knows ultimately that we do his bidding.

I have said to him: "It sounds as though this is your kingdom." He quickly replied: "Isn't it? Of course it is."

I would be awfully sorry if he went away, because one of my great exercises would be over. There is a very real need for him. When I get a message delivered to me from my control personalities, as Dr. Jule Eisenbud[7] has commented, it is rather on the level of "goodness". Dr. Eisenbud made this observation when he stated that most of the messages delivered through mediums such as Mrs. Piper and Mrs. Leonard and myself were all on a rather sanctimonious note.

A little devout these messages perhaps, but the "Noble Stranger" is not "devout" and my profanity amuses him, I think. Yes, I would be very unhappy if he went away. He is intelligent; he tells me ways to look at life, which I don't always understand, and then suddenly one day these concepts seem to be coalesced and I become aware of what he has meant. For, finally, it turns my attention toward the nobility of being. He is the noblest creature I can conceive of.

I very often stop into a church and make prayers for different people to the saints, yet I never experience this same feeling of nobility in Church that I experience while conversing with him.

---

[7] An American psychiatrist and psychical researcher, best known for his books *The World of Ted Serios* (1967), and *Parapsychology and the Unconscious* (1992).

All Are Readying for My Kingdom

I have always had a great sense of horror contemplating the ability of one man sending another man to his doom. I am very sad for our lack of charity and have, for years, sought to support those who have been sent from life by the electric chair or any other of our brutal ways. I have implored him: "Where is the modern right and wrong of this? Has one man the right to say that another man should lose his life? Which is guilty?"

He answered: "He who judges his brother that he must put the crime of society on his brother's shoulders that he may bear it alone, must suffer the wrong too."

"How long will this one suffer?"

He asks: "Which one are you talking about? The one that has been pushed out of life or the one that has taken upon himself this sin against his brother?" He will expound and state: "No man has the right to take the life of a brother, but this will continue, for man is an animal, also. Yes, there will be many who will watch and pray, and there will be many who will feel that justice has been done."

This can be very confusing but finally it falls into shape. I once asked: "What about this generation's troubled teenagers?"

And he says: "They will survive. They will have another opportunity, millions of opportunities."

I ask, "But what about justice?"

"Ah well, all are readying for my kingdom."

Man Has Desecrated Nature

He confuses me. He has questions to answer and he is oracular, completely so. He has very little time for our laws and ethics; he says we have practically none. He pities the other animals that have to live with us. He says we do shocking things to all of nature and nature is weakened, which is apparent when one begins to note the desecrations we bring about in our world.

"Finally, man has desecrated Nature which is so pure and ultimately has desecrated himself."

The awful truth he forces me to confront is that we are ourselves the Devil and that we have such a very long way to travel. I ask: "When will the Church stop us?"

And he replies: "Oh that gathering of unholy brethren. Without them I wouldn't have any fun at all."

We Must Have Sacrifice

I suspect that my "agonies" and conflicts about the Church really come from him in a sense. You see, I don't know how much of the devil is Eileen Garrett and how much Eileen Garrett is devil. I don't know when I could have made him up. I have tried to consider when he first came to me in childhood, but I only have my dream memories. Why do I keep him so separate and apart from my control personalities? I am not afraid of him, but I refuse to permit him to get the better of me, which he well could. He tries to do so when acting soft and appealing; he waits for me to be "touched" and beguiled in his fashion and this is why I get so cross because he has many, many ways to tempt me.

I might be susceptible to his wiles; this is why sometimes I snap at him and deny him and insist: "I am not interested... and you know I am not."

He goes away for a time saying: "Yes, I think I can leave you for a while. You are not in any danger."

I don't anticipate whatsoever by a day or even hours his appearances, as they tend to occur unexpectedly. I never know what will happen with a telephone call, or what a letter may reveal to me. I never know any more than does the sun know if a cloud will obscure his vision; nor does he seem to care. I have nothing planned, but one thing quite unexpected may prompt a chain of questioning within myself and then I think, "I will have to take that up with my friend one of these days." I invariably say "one of these days." I don't say when. I may even have forgotten the particular episode and one day, I may be walking alone—wondering, thinking, trying to understand the meaning of life, the meaning of identity, of holiness, the whole meaning of his words—and suddenly, he appears; and I feel happy for I can't imagine anyone else with whom I would rather spend an hour even if it is an embattled debate.

But, I continue to wonder if he is a part of me. Have I in some way chosen myself, given myself an exalted position—one of being selected for just such dialogues? I don't know. I have been puzzling about the universe since the day I was born. I do not know the answers, and yet I continually look for these answers. I may have been chosen in some way. Why? Why should my two controls[8] have chosen me to work through? Why should the "Noble Stranger" have chosen me to speak with? Why not with the Pope? Why not with Nikita Khrushchev? Why not with plain Joe Doakes?

I have already asked him about the Resurrection, the Temptation, and the Prophets, and how they received this knowledge; about the different gods and the Pantheon of Guardians. I have asked him about all these things. Sometimes he gives me answers which do not please me. I do not tell him I do not immediately agree; I consider his statements and think about them. Perhaps this is the way that I have structured a path for myself to greater understanding.

How can I define my mental state during such experiences? I do not feel a slowing down of my mental activity, but absolutely the reverse. I am completely stimulated, completely in harmony with everything around me. I have weathered some tough battles with him, which is no doubt very important for my development. He is important to me. I have to know myself but what self? The

---

[8] Garrett is here referring to her main controls, Uvani and Abdul Latif. This suggests that she wrote this section prior to her sittings with Ira Progoff (see note 3, above) when Tahoteh "the Giver of the Word" and Ramah "the Giver of Life" first appeared.

self that was there from the beginning? Where did this entity come from? What conceived of this entity, me, in relation to other entities? What is the meaning of the whole pattern? Few have either the time or the interest to answer questions like these. In a strange way, I feel more related to life after we have had our encounters.

No one in my life has offered me as much stimulation. I enjoyed and valued the company of Hewat McKenzie[9], Angus MacDougall[10], Waldemar Kaempffert[11], and Sir Oliver Lodge[12] because of the "authority" with which they tackled the whole of life, being men for whom I have a deep and abiding respect for their wholeness and sympathy for others.

They were not in any way romantic, nor saintly people, but they were very intelligent and humorous. They had a depth of character that carried conviction. I look upon them as the only "masters" I know, and for all of them I have a deep and lasting affection. But I also have affection for my friends, Voodun practitioners encountered out there in the jungles of Haiti, or wherever I meet them, and for him who suddenly says: "You are at it again. I wouldn't waste your time pondering over Algeria at the moment, if I were you. It could become a colony now, but you know, men wouldn't be happy that way, without bloodshed. We could sit down and solve it if there be six good men and true, to get together unselfishly to solve it. But everybody would

---

[9] James Hewat McKenzie (1869–1929), a British psychologist and parapsychologist, was Garrett's mentor at the College of Psychic Science, which he founded.

[10] Angus McDougall was the son of British psychologist and psychical researcher, William McDougall (1871-1938).

[11] Waldemar Kaempffert (1877-1956) was an American popular science writer and member of the American Society for Psychical Research.

[12] Oliver Lodge (1851-1940) was a British physicist and important figure in the early days of the Society for Psychical research, especially for his investigations into the mediumship of Leonora Piper.

have to put his hand in his pocket and give back what he holds, and nobody is willing to do this. We must have sacrifice. We must have bloodshed."

I plead: "But why does it have to happen that way?"

He answers: "Dear child, because man likes it that way."

Well, surely you can never seek to get rid of a fellow who talks like this.

Virile Seducer

I do not believe he thinks I truly have a mind. I really don't think that he regards women as having minds. I asked him long ago: "What is serpent worship?" I think it had come up after I had been in Haiti and I was so impressed with the Dambala[13] worship, the first principle in the Garden of Eden.

He replied: "It is the worship of the phallus, of course, or creation."

"You were there then, in the Garden of Eden?"

"Yes, in every Garden of Eden."

"There are so many?"

"Yes, these two halves of creation joined together for the brief moment through the phallus. Man has set it up as the image of his own divinity and the image of his own creative power."

"Is it also the image of his own intelligence?"

"No, feeling, need and emotion enter at this point; reflection comes afterwards."

I strive to maintain my own identity, as he does not seem to agree that a woman has an identity.

This is yet another basis for our arguments. I do not want to be seduced by him; I would be "lost" with him more than with anyone else. To be lost with him means that one would give up

---

[13] A serpent-spirit and creator in West African and related diaspora religions. Garrett is here associating him with the serpent that tempted Eve in the book of Genesis.

something that one does not quite understand. That is what I suspect a woman is supposed to do under such circumstances— surrender. I don't know; in an affair of the heart or the soul or the mind or the body, I have given myself up to an endless search. I can surrender myself sexually with my heart, but where I wonder am I going at the moment of surrender?

Could it be different if the "Noble Stranger" were involved? I need to reflect deeply on that. I think it is a very important concept to think about: why would I never have in my fantasies thought of myself in the arms of the devil? I never have. The devil, on the whole, is a sort of very masculine symbol: very much the virile seducer. One has read so in literature, but in my relations with him, my seduction hasn't occurred to me. Is he a compensation for what I have not found in other men? That could be, because the men I like are somewhat identified with sensuality, non-aggressive; not necessarily weak, but idealistic. Yes, it could be, only he has not weakness, but much cynicism.

He usually turns up looking very well dressed, wearing the right kind of male attire, the right kind of shoes that gives you the idea that he has long slender feet, his face is haggard but the eyes are hypnotic and therefore compelling. All in all, he presents a rich measure of stimulating vitality. I have kept celibate from time to time, as I noticed during the early process of mediumship visitations and visions I was entering into states of ecstasy and, one would say, orgiastic ecstasy. I began to find then in myself that for much of my traveling, when I went mentally to seek friends, when I had visions, much of my telepathic "traveling" brought to me a desire to depart from the field of sexual endeavor alone. I then must have in some way interfered with the whole process of my menstruation, because when I worked in mediumship, I would go for long periods without menstruating.

This was the first clue I had to the fact that my menstrual period time was a "low" point in my mediumship. After working for about five years as a medium, I was very relieved and delighted to find that, although I had pains and aches relative to the monthly flow, I did not have any appearance of blood. I then went so far as to take cold baths around the rhythmic period, in order not to have this interference, because I found the menstrual flow produced a low level of intellect and work, and I thought how much more constructive it would be to finish with it altogether.

I relate this to what transpired when I spoke about my "Noble Stranger." I was resolved to be finished with the feminine problems of process, although I had no idea why this was considered important. I realized the need to sublimate sex, and finally in the days of my College of Psychic Science experiences, when my work with sitters was all-important, I would sublimate it so that I would have only infrequent sexual relations.

I was indeed fond of my last husband, William Garrett. I had a wonderful relationship with him but not on a physical level at all. Finally he pointed this out to me and I realized that, much as I liked him as a friend, he was no longer acceptable as a lover. I entered into spontaneous research of my own to see what I really liked about sex with any man, and I realized that what I wanted was just to have a very quick, sudden and passionate "disheveled" affair, especially happy to have no identity with a man that mattered.

I recall that when I was widowed during the First World War, I used to go to dinner at the Berkeley Hotel with friends, men in uniform. They would suggest: "Eileen, we would like you to meet 'so and so'", and I would reply: "Never divulge his name to me," because if I had made up my mind that someone would be acceptable as a sex symbol, if I knew him on a level of closeness, I would cease to be interested.

I have related this characteristic in myself to the mystical need and transmutation of my energies to the mystical area. I could dream about somebody whose name I didn't know, or think that one day I might meet him again, without having any previous relationship to his history or home destination. I could thus get real enjoyment and magic out of sex.

The sex act finally became for me a means and ways of finding a way to God. It became holy, and I think I have scared lovers by my mystical exaltation at such moments when they seem to wonder what had happened to me when I became nonchalant. I realized that I was using sex as a method of escape, that I never gave much "partnership." This comes as an interesting insight as to why I say I assume I would be "lost" if I had any kind of relations with the devil. I would lose my identity.

There is a form of orgiastic energy in mediumship. The years that I spent in the College were, of course, given over to the trance personalities, so this was an aspect of death. Every sexual relationship that I had became a form of dying, dying in the physical sense of the word, and if I didn't get this experience of exultation out of it, it didn't really mean anything to me and I was consequently quite disappointed and sad. Trance communications, in my own mind, may also be a form of dying.

Sex and mediumship, I think, are related. Not only in the sense that sex is related to everything we do in life, to all our appetites; but also that we are able alchemists and can turn sex energy into many other levels of experience.

I learned at a very early age the great necessity for so doing. My drive to work is related very much to my need to deal with sex in a constructive and highly evolved fashion. I know that if one simply gives way to the appetites of sex, one can be subordinated by it, and since I have a sense of purity about sex, as well as a sense of mysticism about it, I cannot help feeling that I have regarded it in an entirely different fashion from most women.

My first sexual relationship was a purely mystical one. I envisioned a relationship in my mind that could only be used in the highest sense, as the act for the creation of children. It seemed to me then to be the means to an end, and during my first years when I became pregnant, I also had a sense that to have sexual relations during pregnancy was almost a profanity.

I "elevated" sex to a mystical relationship, which may have in some way made the step from sex to mediumship very easy for me because, having had a terrific amount of energy, I unconsciously knew it was not arrived at by logical means, but that I must have for myself many, many subjective activities in order to keep myself always occupied.

After the birth of my children, perhaps I came to an animal enjoyment of sex, but then something else revealed itself to me. I was using it with terrific curiosity. I wanted to see where I went during the act, and at the moment of high exultation it became important for me to forget my partner, and very often I lost all contact with him. I realized very soon that I was using this as a search. I then hardly used it at all for long periods.

I once commented on someone who had married an acquaintance that one of the attractions about this woman was that she was treating sex like food and drink, something that is quite natural, quite animalistic. I spoke of this with a sense of envy, a sense of appreciation of what was quite different from my own point of view of what sex should be. What is this "ambivalence?" I don't know.

Food and drink give me little pleasure. I really think that some of my many illnesses may be due to the fact that in certain areas I have cut myself off from enough proper sustenance. For years I have had no real appreciation of food, any more than I have any real appreciation of sex on a purely physical level.

For me, the ceremony leading up to the sexual act is important. The only time I really dress beautifully is when I dress for bed and seduction. I have always made a fetish of how I shall appear in the room of my husband or lover, yet I have always taken very good care also to get myself out of that room back to my own domain.

I have never been able to understand the sheer delight of lying in any man's arms or bed after the sexual act is completed, or even in being in close contact with him bodily; but then, I am also very strange about touching people.

I touch people to heal, but in my sentimental relationships, I am not very keen on touch at all, and certainly never have been a woman who has had to have any help or any excitation before the sex act. In that way, I presume I am really very masculine. I may have been suppressing my femininity when

I was unconsciously trying to stop menstruating. I have always wondered why I did it, but it is quite obvious as I look back at the situation now, that I must have always in a sense resented being feminine and yet outwardly and physically, I think I am in fact very feminine. I think in most of the aspects of my dealing with people I am not in the least aggressive.

I would be very interested to learn, through analysis, what was it that has made me feel always so mystical in the sex act. Unless I could find the kind of esthetic male who looked beautiful, was beautiful, and could be used purely as a method and means in which I could be transported to a transcendental level—a level often beyond his understanding—the level that often upsets the male who wants to be assured that he is loved—I had only been selfishly "motivated" to discover something in the exalted mood, the search for God.

These themes: holiness, search for God, purity, mysticism—none of these could sex could fulfill as well as non-sexual exultation. But mediumship is not the sort of thing that leads to exultation; it leads to a resemblance of death; it leads to a withdrawal, an oblivion. It is oblivion.

But the mystical experience outside of trance is something different. It can overtake me at any time; I feel I am contained in space into invisible arms. I say "the arms of"—and I have always asked myself what do I mean by it without knowing, but I always feel that there is a part of the universe that can envelop me in symbolism.

I have got these two spirals always working to keep me moving upward and downward, beyond and outward. I have come to regard these spirals as arms, universal arms through which I am able at all times to get my evidence and answers. So the mystical exaltation that I get so often leaves me as I would be left if I had given myself over entirely and completely on a romantic level. I am suspended. My heart is beating. I sometimes have palpitation, and I am completely outside of time.

The Universal Polarity

One morning our dialogue was on the question of "Man's theology." Lucifer advised me that in every civilization, it is brought about by the influence of their time. It appears true that man "cannot live by bread alone."

The living breath demands answers from the stars, the moon, the sun and the elements; each in their time have been deified. The sense of belonging to the "heavenly" bodies and elements can be understood. The elements that give fecundity and sustenance to man and all of life cannot be ignored. The "incarnations" of fire, air, water, and earth have apparently played powerful parts in our thoughts from the beginning. Lucifer advised me that this cosmic pulse, which draws upon the "vital cause", must be taken into account.

The "Noble Stranger" shared with me that the votaries of Mithra, like the ancient Persians, adored the sun: a chariot in space, which sank into the water with evening's approach. This becomes a purifying element in all life, to take away and restore. New peoples arose seeking forever new elements in nature—man's growth and vision made the simpler religions difficult to harmonize with their own life cycle. So we have the rationalism of one oriental group as opposed to the paganism of the other, which is illustrated for us in the Story of Moses, when Moses led the children of Israel out of the desert.

It is little wonder that the heavenly bodies were identified and worshipped. The twelve signs of the Zodiac in their revolutions through the "heavenly" spheres were thought to influence people. Each of the signs was venerated, grouped in threes according to the season to which they conformed. The signs of the Zodiac, he informed me, were not the only constellations to be incorporated; he referred with some seriousness to my being deeply moved during my own visits to Greece and Crete by the worship of Mithra surrounded with the Zodiac, but also the moon's chariot drawn by bulls. The mysteries were thus freely "translated" to give and to embrace all possible sources of energy. The mysteries were man's definite need for spiritual sustenance combined with his knowledge. The Zodiac, Lucifer points out, preserves its incontestable primary powers among "astrologists" of the day.

I spoke of pain—not to ask his help, but to get his comments. He informed me that "Pain and sacrifice are a part of evolution. The reflective mind knows that 'they' help the growth of soul through experience." Without my numerous illnesses, he instructs me, I would not have had the *identification* with the suffering of others that marks my life. It is an antidote also to what man calls evil—for the man that has suffered is likely to call upon his own powers when "simples and potions" no longer sustain him.

"It has its justification in your life. Not 'demons' but the need for greater strength has been your 'aberrations' if you want to hold this word to you. If you were to set aside the order and discipline that have entered your life by this channel, the growth of your being might have been subdued. Though you speak of many Gods, you do so with tenderness, and this is just, for they have been made in the image of man, his ancestors, and the elements all powerful! All mysteries have freely condoned and taught man those aspects of prayer, both for discipline and to give him a sense of the 'magical' qualities of his universe. Without these conceptions of a superior being, demons, and malevolent spirits, man in his early stages would not be competent to survive or believe that there were benevolent powers at work, supplementing and supporting his expanding efforts. It is the universal polarity at work within each and all!

"Man must have a hero! Look at the growth of remarkable hero-worship within your own epoch. Unfortunately, your heroes are today not contained in the celestial atmosphere and so they cease to be heroes too quickly when youth can no longer emulate and outstrip them in their efforts. Your present-day heroes are not 'intermediaries' given to esoteric doctrines, which offer the sacred symbol which man needs to sustain him.

Man must measure his strength against the unobtainable; he must be able to render homage to the untouchable."

I am impressed by the sense of inevitability—destiny, if you will—contained in these dialogues. I asked him about the worship of the bull, and sacrifice. "This arose a long time ago, when shepherds and the men who tilled the land, as well as hunters, knew that wealth was derived from their flocks. (You still have the image of the Lamb within your Christian theology). The captor of a wild bull necessary to propagate the flocks needed vision and ingenuity. The hero who conquered the animal was thought to be a visionary who had been given peculiar strength to conquer, slay, and drag such an animal to his cave providing sustenance. This undertaking illustrated the human suffering that took place in the struggle, but if the bull escaped, as it often did, to roam his wild pastures, he rendered himself stronger than man and therefore would be respected, and one day deified, and finally sacrificed to the greater elements."

He continued to expound: "Today I note that you have departed into a world where a like act will sustain and cheer the multitude. These new men often became famous and are, in a sense, made 'holy'; only now you carry your emotions to excess, to expend them without thought as to the rigid discipline that made these men who ride the wind and the currents of the ocean, or climb the mountains, different. Vision and discipline—resistance to this form of sensual worship—was the duty of the Priests who must maintain and foster the need for individual effort in the young, and help to develop like powers in the human mind; it was ever thus." He disappeared on this note.

Garments of the Soul

On another visit, he spoke of the "garments of the soul" that have to be shed. And so, he told me: "You have abandoned to the moon your vital energy as you watch it through the night and lose your sleep. To Venus, you dedicate appetites that you feel are part of her being and yours; to Mercury, desires for vision; to the Sun, for blessings, for warmth and life; to Mars, your aggressions; to Jupiter and Saturn, your inclinations to know more and penetrate their mysteries. These are your prayers, your identification with the unknown, and in return for these aspects, they stir or arouse you to receive the eternal vision—light if you so desire—to make you feel you bathe in the beatitude of the Gods. The happiness reserved for a nomad like you in the spiritual world is hard for others to conceive, for these reflections are difficult for other minds to conceive. Theology, therefore, with its 'thou shalt nots' is at once naïve and artificial. The vigor of the ethics, which is concerned with order in these celestial states, cannot be estimated, for these are powerful forces that you look to for stimulus and support. Throughout the growth of life, there have been those who believe themselves helped and sustained by celestial powers which, in many cases, have made them powerful zealots, even pious frauds."

The "Noble Stranger" comes at no one's bidding—only occasionally to answer the questions of Professor Servadio. Perhaps he is a personification built up through the years of the "ideal comrade," who knows about my curious affinity for the stars, the wind that stirs the leaves gently and yet produces turbulence and disorder. I have come to think of him as the spirit of the babbling brook and there is a sense of him having a different nature from man that provokes a feeling of awe and yet of well-being. He is the leader of the ritual in which I have deep interest—the unknown melodies out of the past! He is the Greek and Alexandrian epoch; he hints of ancient and barbaric things. He is the spirit of ancient Gods and ancient usage, which compels me to look for him within the mysteries. He is the one who conceived the blood sacrifice by which man seeks purity. He is not to be known as father, brother or leader, and there are no incantations to be made to call him. He wears neither crown nor sword. Perhaps I found him out of some Gnostic pattern when I worked in the early days of my mediumship with G.R.S. Mead, himself a student of ancient rites, a great Gnostic and secretary to theosophy's Madame Blavatsky. I do nothing to serve the "Noble Stranger", and have no knowledge of how I would serve him if I could. Is he indeed Lucifer incarnate? He has no relation to Christian theology, for he bears no likeness to my young "traditions" about Lucifer. His alterations in physique are subtle, to be felt rather than described; "Lucifer," he named himself on the occasion when I sought to give him a name!

Storm and Tranquility

For approximately two years I had no contact with the "Noble Stranger" that was outside of the boundary of imagination. My last contact with him prior to the cessation of his visits was under the sensory deprivation of an LSD experience, when I sought him in the darkness of the night while in Florida. He appeared to me as a Priest in white, or one who worshipped, and later monk-like in opaque clothing.

No one can explain to me the meaning of this session, though I have discussed it with several learned academicians and psychoanalysts. They seem to believe that I may have sunk deeply into the primordial aspects of the world of life. There, I saw him in the height of this experience, dressed in white, withdrawn and watchful. Was he a source therefore of purity, and is purity portrayed in white in my own mind? He was aloof. Two hours later, I saw him again, more haggard and monk-like in an opaque robe, neither white nor grey. He looked at me as though he knew I had gone through some kind of initiation, which, indeed, I had. He was neither pagan nor Christian, but he provoked in me a sense of reverential awe for an august mystery. Good or God, Saint or Monk, or deep primordial image—I cannot make up my mind. They are all aspects of growth. Perhaps I am never to know.

LSD is ecstasy for me. By the sea I am almost compelled to throw myself in its arms, but to do this I know would be folly. Had I taken LSD when young, I would have written the song of the waves and what their masters, the currents and winds, whisper and shout to them in tranquility and violence. Observing the endless urgency of the sea lashed by the hurricane force, I am moved myself by the forces in nature that possess, compel and cleanse. It is like being present when gladiators wrestle; I get caught, possessed, almost compelled by the power of the elements; I catch my breath with sobs. I am overcome with the force of the ecstasy, until I seem not to have more power or place in my lungs for expansion. It would be wonderful then to take LSD again and find new words to praise the turmoil of the winds and the water. One could aspire to be a poet, but the words could never do justice—a woman can feel the majesty within, but it needs a man's will to write poetry. Part of air and sunlight—surely pain and pleasure—are not a woman's way to words.

I can actually see the spiraling forms of the wind's energy like great windmill arms sweeping out and around to embrace, hold, and change the leaves and seeds, feathery floss from the waves, flotsam from the sand; all caught together to lose their initial uniqueness, become as dust before the storm—yet still to merge within the life cycle. When this happens to me, my whole body burns with excitement to ache and hurt, but afterwards, I feel empty of thought.

Therefore, the inhibiting factor of LSD in the brain allows the body to "play" with the elements in nature. It is like a prolonged bath where one has been freed from the mundane. This is, indeed, ecstasy! As a child, I escaped to roll in the snow until my body burned with the cold. That, too, was ecstasy, as was the punishment that followed such actions.

What of my walks in the overgrown Floridian jungle under the influence of LSD? I find trees with which I have a particular affinity; I lean against them, and soon I am breathing in their rhythm. It is then that I see them as they are, native to the earth. I reflect on their change, now growing out of jungle mud, and see the place around as a mass of growth's energy. If they have come from the countries I clairvoyantly "know," their ancient lands, I can sigh with them for now they are as slaves to a new terrain; forever caught, for their feet are firmly fitted in an alien land, but like humans, they have memories of their own beginnings.

I am often recalled from their dreams, and being part of the fantasy, by a voice in the distance calling me back. Perhaps the wind has carried to me someone's call to return.

Would I want to be water and wind—formless? Would I like to throw myself into the water and, if I would, isn't all this a fantasy of suicide? I don't think it is a suicidal wish at all. I have never wanted to finish my life before its allotted time, but I know that within my body the seeds of life and death fight out their battles continually. I know I have envied skin divers, their feeling of euphoria under water, and while I love to be in water, sit by it, know its "qualities," I have no desire to have my life stop within its folding caress! I know that the rhythm of the sea beats in my own blood; ancient memories are stirred; the long circle of evolution has not deadened the relationship between my blood and the sea.

What about my feelings for the "Noble Stranger"? They are different. I have another kind of excitement about him. Perhaps there are in his image the elements of life that bring storm and tranquility. I am always torn between the world of happenings and the cool or tempestuous routes of nature; I prefer to reflect rather than talk. This kiss of the moods of nature has a sensuality that I find tranquil, peace giving; yet not all nature's moods are tranquil and majestic. But so I think is the "Noble Stranger."

All this may be sexual, though I hardly think so. If you refer to the act it can be brief, and not to be shared with one other. But on the other hand, all of these feelings may fulfill the sensual side of my nature. The act of sex is giving, but though I am, in a sense possessed by the elements and also *impressed* by the appearance of this "Noble Stranger/Lucifer" figure, these are different levels of experience that hold me in their embrace. They are all different levels of sensuality, but each and all give me a sense of participation. Perhaps some of my dreams of him have a sexual content because he represents somebody with whom I could be very content. I am not by nature physically very taken in by any sexual impulse. I take. I regard sex as a means and ways of reaching the Infinite Intelligence.

To each mood there is certainly an abandonment of self, but on many subtle levels. The theosophists speak of seven bodies or levels of experience. I think there could be seventy-seven, or seven thousand—who knows? When I rode a motorbike, rode horseback, drove motorboats, they were related. They were all related to hurtling through the wind. One is riding through currents of air that whips one; one is not thinking. One is in the mood to give and accept. There is an acute exhilaration in all of these, and one has an aloneness that appeals to one. In love, one is not alone. The melody is a dual affair, and much depends on the partner's ability to understand love. But the other activities can be one's love affair with the currents of life, even destiny.

Let the Gods Decide

Alcohol is for me a social experience. Without the empathy of friends, it has no meaning. I like two drinks—even a third at times—but no more. Once my mental faculties get loosened, I do not feel happy. I must always keep my head. I have been in the habit of taking more sedatives than most other people, for I have been the victim of surgery so often, and other ills from childhood on. They may one and all have a tranquilizing effect, but I somehow get above them and have no feeling for any of the medication used in the hospital. I did once take opium in Marseille in 1936 when I had a great deal of pain with pneumonia and the heart, but far from getting me to sleep, I got a racing pulse and for two hours had a delightful "out-of-the-body" experience with the painter, Gauguin. His work I naturally find violent, but under the effects of opium I understood perfectly. When I was quiet, I asked Gaugin "Shall I see you again?"

"Yes," he said, "providing you use opium."

I haven't done so, having never felt an impulse to take opium on my own accord.

Do I never surrender? Yes and no! I participate but I cannot give my will. In hypnosis, I will to use myself and *give* myself, but then I have practiced autohypnosis for half my life span. I give myself over to LSD and psilocybin and those elements in nature that give me vision, recollection, speculation, reflection and finally, answers.

As elements, I know that the Gods exist for me—perhaps as fate, a pattern of the overtones of life and destiny. As such, I salute them. Long ago I have learned that pain and suffering give patience and tolerance, even to an independent woman as I am. They are taskmasters, but also charitable. I believe in my Haitian pantheon, and saints also. Why not? Others do. Since God or good is all-powerful, all his agents must share his beneficence. They do for me. I can be forceful and forthright in making decisions, and yet I say: "let the Gods decide." My brain is my own, my responsibility for making decisions as to right and wrong—these are my responsibilities; but in the larger measure of life, where charity, nobility and grace belong, I give the gods their dues; this is my right.

Both the Tempter and the Tempted

I have never asked the help of the "Noble Stranger" in pain or to help make decisions. My need for him relates to world affairs, theology, symbolism, meaning contained within meanings. My private identity with pain is the body's affair, and must be understood, balanced and lived with for the needs of others, and for my own ability to work with and through it. I can cut discomfort and pain with work. I can forget it when I am caught up in thoughtfulness and creative action. "What are you looking for always?" he asks me. The meaning of God, good, charity, and to what end is life my purpose. These are true aspects not especially related to dogma, but to life as one lives it daily.

Motivation and purpose go hand in hand—and the dynamic principle of being moves me like a chess piece within the hands of the player. During a recent visit from Lucifer we talked about this dynamic principle of being always in the "now," looking ahead and never glancing backward for yesterdays. I once gave a sitting to a lady whose whole life was lived looking backwards. We discussed this. "This," he told me, "is a form of death of mind, of imagination. It is too much of a pattern by now, and one you cannot change. Let her go with her dead dreamer. It is too late to change her." I queried if one is never too late? "Perhaps not as you see life, but if the windows of the soul are not kept open, the sudden light of orientation may enter, not to change, but to confuse! Your misplaced attitude toward 'changing people for the better' rarely works. She is indoctrinated, a creature of habit; seek to destroy her habits when they are well formed and you leave her bereft!"

I came to understand that knowledge is arrived at by perception, reflection, deduction, and comparison. He who looks back becomes unready to bend the will of the mind. Ethics have come to be regarded as living within the conformity of law and society, but this is not so. Ethical behavior stems from the inner sense of knowledge—of being at peace with oneself within the norm of society. He remarks rather sagely: "Do not look for it within governments or religion. Man's greed for power has caused the meaning to be changed!" Should ethics then be concerned with dogmas? No, dogmas should be concerned with ethics and moral adjustments.

I asked the "Noble Stranger" if he could be described as eternal? "Unfortunately!" he replied. He does not speak of conflict; he uses the word thoughtfully especially when he speaks of education, which he terms "instruction," He is often sardonic about "methods" of education. He does not refer to any one particular man, well known in the world of state, economics or politics, as being a model for "our time," for he will pay no man highly placed in these areas the compliment of being a role model. "His" good men and true are the few poets and painters who create from within themselves. The others, he insists, are "power-driven, whether they will it or not, and open to a variety of temptations." He finds our civilization difficult, and comments that we take no time to understand the imbalance that we create for life, as trees, plants and animals suffer to lose out and die because of us. "We cannot take the human animal into account," he tells me, "his sins against the planet are a cause of eternal sadness."

"But," I have suggested many times to him "are you not the alleged cause of all this?"

He answers: "I am both the tempter and the tempted."

Light to Lead the Way

How about evil? He says man's idea of evil changes with his "attitude" toward his chosen Deity of the time, as do his symbols. "What you call evil in your day has no meaning other than that given by your dogmas which are invariably there to serve the powerful, whether in church or state. The building up of good and evil are attachments to form the highest nature: omnipresent, silent, mysterious, growing from the polarity of its own being. What you enter at birth is fullness and complete, but as you grow within your time and epoch, the polarities of being continue to appear to make choices for you—as you swing from pole to pole in achievement—hence, experience. Mind contains the time clock by which the hours will be measured as the river of mind passes through the body. Evil, as you term one of the poles of being, is no more than the opening force of what you call good. Within each is the cosmic pattern of your destiny."

"But God," I ask him, "is the great opposite to Lucifer?"

"No," he told me. "Lucifer is light to lead the way over the territory to be traversed—your destiny will do the rest, whether you tread heavily or gaily on the route to self-knowledge, gained by what man is pleased to call evil and good. What you call evil and good are the dynamic methods of mind's sensory perception, 'timing' the mind to order, to form, and experience. Without these polarities, there can be no motivation in life—no growth."

Guard the Uniqueness of You

Until the age of thirty I did not dwell very much on his sporadic appearances. I then experienced a very serious breakdown in health. I wasn't prepared to take the necessary rest and recuperate. I wasn't prepared to obey all the dictums of concerned doctors and friends as to what I now could or could not do and how it would benefit my recovery if I did this or that.

One night I saw, sitting by my bed, while I was in a moment of deep distress, this very beautiful creature. He reached out to touch me and I said, "It's you. Where have you been?"

He answered me, "So far from you and yet, at times, so near to you."

"Why haven't I seen you?"

"You have been caught in other things."

"Why have you come?"

"To tell you that the things that you have been told to do are not for you. Guard the uniqueness of you—the you. Rest is never rest. Only change is rest."

I responded: "Whenever you come, you always say something that hits at the core. You set me off looking into all these series of other people's religions. You set me thinking about life and sun."

He questioned "The Son of God? Or the Son of Man?"

I answered him, "Neither, just the sun of life."

He said: "Wisely said. Now take my word and believe me that you will do best to follow the dream, the way that is for you."

I asked: "Will you come back?" to which he answered: "I never go away. Unfortunately, I am bound to this."
"To me?"
"Oh, no!"
"To yourself?"
"Yes, most of all. To God—wholly." As I have come to expect, he disappeared.

The Subhuman World

Another occasion on which he revealed himself transpired when I was living through certain experiences during my early mediumship work at the British College of Psychic Science. It was a period of being seemingly transported for quite some time into barren areas where I saw strange plants, lichens and shrubs, all living on each other—none of them dangerous to me as I perceived them, but very lusty in their desire to accumulate experience, to live, to hurry.

I also experienced what I termed a sub-human world, because I would not speak of it to anyone. While there, I saw a very strange people—some very tall, like giants that you see in a circus, ill-formed; some small, as midgets; some whose arms or legs hadn't grown to a normal size; all of them in agony. And yet, although they made me feel very uncomfortable and I hated to return to them, I had no real fear *per se*. My feelings would be better described as trepidation and awe.

Having lived with this subhuman world for approximately two years, I might get up very early in the morning to watch the sunrise and find one of its denizens on the lawn. I might go to the bottom of the garden and find another one. I came to the conclusion that I was being haunted—haunted, for want of a better word, by leprechauns, "the little people" of Irish mythology.

It is interesting that I never saw the feminine form in this scenario. They were all male; not that I noticed anything in their physical makeup that led me to identify specifically a male child or male adult. One understood their masculinity from their vitality, but as far as I can remember I never saw actual male features. Because they were so ugly and misshapen, they aroused my compassion.

I would encounter them in bunches at night. I used to hug my dog, a Sealyham terrier, at these moments, very close to me and I would use him as an anchor onto which I could cling in the event that I found myself once again entering their stunted sub-human world. There was no sunlight; there was graylight. I looked for stars and the moon as well as for our sun but could find none in this world. They were enveloped in a gray atmosphere. Sometimes I saw them through fog and sometimes through a weird light akin to what sometimes appears before a very violent storm. This very eerie type of atmosphere did not frighten me, yet compelled me to look directly at these poor creatures.

It was only occasionally that one or other of them stepped out of the picture in daylight or twilight or early morning light and then sometimes I would picture a very great giant and a very little creature. Sometimes I saw them as though I were looking into a crèche, or nursery, where their limbs had not yet appeared; as one sees along New York's famed Broadway beggars without arms and legs. This filled me with a terrific compassion, but it also filled me with a sense that perhaps I was slowly but surely going mad. And to whom could I share these visions? I felt it had nothing whatever to do with the spiritualist theory in which I was compelled to work within the College. I didn't think I could go to my long-time friend, G.R.S. Mead. Finally, I didn't go to anybody. I feared talking about these experiences.

Then one night I suddenly thought, if I could only find the "Noble Stranger" I could ask him. But as that idea formulated I immediately thought of the futility of asking about something so bizarre. Perhaps they were only hallucinations.

Surprisingly, he appeared as always with his same very sad, concrete and noble features. I implored him: "My God, where have you been."

And he replied: "Your God? Now who is your God?"

I answered: "But what has that to do with it? I need your explanation."

"Why my explanation?"

"Because I don't know anybody else who can divert me." I then asked, "What is the meaning of this terrifying experience through which I have gone?"

He said: "I once told you to get interested in the productive elements of life and not to waste time on things that you don't really need. I have tried to show you—I have tried to show you, let me emphasize this—a sub-human world because, you see, life must go through many experiences.

"Man, before he becomes man, must go through many experiences. From the grain of sand, that which becomes man must perhaps for countless millions of centuries, under the ground, in the stone, under the sea, be drifted by the winds blowing here and there from one territory to another. And then, he must grow through mineral to plant and through the countless areas of evolution, always growing in understanding—misunderstanding and understanding. He must also go through all the forms of what is known as hell: struggles, contemptible things in living, where he cannot know himself, where he cannot order himself, where he cannot see himself, and yet where he must finally endure himself."

I asked: "Then I have been looking into forms of hell?"

And he said: "Hell? Heal? Isn't that what you want to do with these people? Well, then, heal them but don't hurry their evolution."

Then I said to him: "Now, we have come to grips. Who are you?"

And he reminded me, "Oh, I am known by many names, you shall call me whatever you like. I have even been known by Lucifer."

I laughed and said: "Oh no, you don't fulfill that role! Where is your tail?"

"Oh," he said, "like the rest of man I have dropped it on the way."

This statement intrigued me greatly and so I asked: "Then men came from monkeys?"

"Well, not *came* from—by way of. Be careful of your phraseology."

And with that he took his leave.

So Charming and So Kind

In 1927, I had broken with the Labor Party after the General Strike. I had seen some of my friends moving to the Communist Movement, which disturbed me. I had been very interested in the Fabian doctrine at this point but I came to the conclusion that all this was not for me. It was around this time that I began to have this stratum of sub-humanism revealed to me. Perhaps this developed during the time of personal turbulence within my political beliefs as I impatiently informed one of Labor's leaders, "Either go out and use your guns and have a revolution, or stop talking about it."

From my earliest day, I can remember leaving the church, even slipping out in the middle of the Protestant service, knowing that Catholic Mass would soon be over and that John Redmond or William O'Brien or one of the great "agitators" would be outside. They voiced such language as one rarely heard and there was an element of violence from the Home Rule enthusiasts. Their violence, their turbulence, and their sincerity had helped to form me at a very early age into a young revolutionary, and a very conscious anarchist in a sense.

I had listened to their speeches from the first day I went to Catholic school, even at the risk of severe scoldings from my uncle, who disapproved of my intent to leave my own Protestant church. He didn't always tell my aunt that I was doing this and in his goodness of heart, would come by the schoolhouse to get me on his way home because I usually forgot meals and everything else being so caught up in the drama of the political structure of Ireland at that time.

With World War I coming to an end, I had found myself in 1918 married to my third husband, after being divorced and widowed, because I wanted to heal him and save his leg from suggested amputation. I had experienced a terrible revolt within myself following Armistice Day in taking up my ordinary life. The bells were ringing the Armistice news out, and on Southampton Road I took a lease of a place that later on became the first Labor hostel in London. Revolution in my heart again in 1926, I left with a feeling that whatever I had learned from my political experiences were not to be a constant in my life.

I had, however, warned my best friends that I was leaving the movement so that it would be less of a shock to them. I had seen Jack Jones of Silvertown, one of the members of the Commons, of whom I was very fond, a really reputable but equally disreputable character. I find it amazing that, in my opinion, no one has penned a good book on him, as he was an excellent fighter. I told him that I was now leaving, and must walk alone. He told me "you have always walked alone in your life as have I."

Thus, I entered a new phase of my life, throwing myself completely and entirely into the study of psychic phenomena, but still affected by my visits in the "sub-human" world. I didn't like these visits but I could not help myself. I *had* to visit, though dreading it and clinging to my dog. I had to go back to them as I felt a compassionate wonder about them, a sorrow for them.

The "Noble Stranger" had said: "Hell … Heal … Heal?" but the thing I always came away with was not the fright or the fact that I needed my dog for company, but that I felt a terrific sympathy and sadness for them. I felt that perhaps my "Noble Stranger" had opened this way for me to understand that there were levels of experience in the deep unconscious which one day I would have to find the meaning of. The meaning of the sub-human stratum has not yet been revealed to me any more than the meaning of the "Noble Stranger," who has indeed become my mentor at all points.

As we have grown to know each other, I have asked him: "But how is it possible, if you are the devil, that you can be so charming and so kind?"

And he said: "I always have known that if you want to get your way, quickly and easily, you can do it better with charm and kindliness." This again for me was a great lesson.

So far, the things he has told me have been constructive. He insists that he came to this planet, not by wish or will, but only through a true desire.

Also Experience

After 1930 I came to the conclusion, after years working as a medium, and with my mentor Hewat McKenzie dead, that this part of my life was over. I also came to the conclusion that I wasn't very good for any man. It was then that I told the "Noble Stranger": "I am going to make a vow to you that I am never going to marry again."

He didn't seem to take any notice and I asked, "Did you hear that?"

He nodded. "You are making a vow to yourself, of course," he said, "not to me."

I went on to state that "Well, whichever way you like it, I will never marry, because through marriage I bring pain and despair."

"Also experience," he said.

"Yes, but perhaps I don't know how to handle experience yet. I am going to leave England, change all my habits, take my daughter with me and start not a new life, but start on a new experience."

Thus, I left for America in early 1931.

Between Good and Good

Our next encounter was three months later, when my disappointment was rising with my work at the American Society for Psychical Research. I felt that they were not taking the work very seriously at Hyslop House. I enjoyed working with Freddy Bligh-Bond[14] because he was receiving messages at this time from some of the old Christian Fathers. I enjoyed some of the work with researchers, but I became deluged with sitters seeking my mediumistic abilities, and while wined and dined and caught up in a great mass of social activity I knew this had little relationship to my work and calling. I was very upset by the whole Marjorie Crandon affair[15] and I was even more upset because I was working within the spiritualist section of the ASPR which I found confining. I was once again mired in mediumship, although I did not think that this would be the case when I had debarked in America.

My work with Drs. Hyslop[16] and Zabriski[17] had been negatively impacted by work going on in Boston with the Crandon case. I despairingly saw no opportunity for me to

---

[14] A British architect, archaeologist, and psychical researcher known for his discoveries at Glastonbury Abbey during the period 1909-1921, alleged to have been guided by spirits of the dead through mediums. A book about the case by William W. Kenawell was later published by Garrett's own Helix Press, *The Quest at Glastonbury: A Biographical Study of Frederick Bligh Bond* (1965).

[15] Mina "Margery" Crandon (1888-1941) was a famous Canadian medium whose claims and abilities were discredited by Harry Houdini, Joseph Banks Rhine, a committee of Harvard scholars, and *Scientific American* magazine.

[16] James Hyslop (1854-1920), Professor of Logic and Ethics at Columbia University, prominent psychical researcher, and important figure in the ASPR.

[17] Edwin G. Zabriskie (1874-1959), an American psychiatrist who was on the board of trustees and the research committee of the American Society for Psychical Research.

do really rigorous scientific research. I became swept up in all the hysteria and complexity of the Lindberg baby kidnapping case, which worried me enormously. I attempted to send for the "Noble Stranger," to no avail for three or four days. When finally he made his appearance, he was quite illuminating but very cross with me.

"Now you have grown up, and must make your own choices. I have shown you the road between good and good."

And I said: "Evil?"

He replied: "I know not evil."

Eagerly I said: "Oh, that interests me—then there is no evil?"

"No, there is the other side of the coin and that is gray."

"Yes, but it has a different inscription?"

"Yes, but it has a relationship to the bright side of the coin."

"Then you are not evil."

"No, only as you can conceive of it."

And then we had a long conversation about the meaning of evil and what it is and I told him, "Well, if I go on like this, then I will be consciously committing evil, because I am going to dinners and functions, mixing with a lot of people and allowing myself to be used in a way which I should not be used. And therefore, if I continue in this manner, it will surely constitute evil—not as evil but as the antithesis of good."

"Then," he said, "if this is your feeling, be on your way."

On another occasion, when I was leaving Hyslop House, I was very upset because having seen the further debacle of the Crandon mediumship I was hurt deeply, fearing that this situation would drastically hurt the path of continued psychical research. I remember standing on the doorstep and saying out loud in case he was near, "Look at the evil that is taking place when money leads to such a sorry spectacle!" And with that, having so to speak, uttered my "black mass" I demanded of him: "Well, how strong *are* you, and what good are you *anyway*?" I flounced off.

A little while later, Freddy Bligh-Bond and Hereward Carrington[18] confessed their part in knowing or suspecting and having their doubts about the truth of the Marjorie mediumship. A purge resulted involving reorganization of the ASPR. I suppose the record will perhaps never truly be revealed. I left, telling the people concerned that I was on my way out of New York to the West Coast of America.

I never thought any more about it. Then, one day, I felt I must go down and visit Hyslop House, and behold it had gone— razed to the ground. So perhaps my friend had played his part as requested.

My Devil Image

The following ten years found me busy in all forms of analysis, in all forms of exploration, in all forms that might be considered the undoing of that structure for which, for the previous ten years, I had given up every day of my life: that is, building up the idea that there could be communication with life after death. I felt confident that I was peculiarly on the right track. I had built up the structure of my mediumship without truly believing in it and now I felt it was for me time to attack it. This is why from 1932-1937, I spent much of my time in analysis and even forgot to a large part my devil image.

As a matter of fact, during those days I even began to tell myself "What rubbish and nonsense all these Lucifer visitations. What was I up to?" I discarded him completely.

---

[18] Hereward Carrington (1880 –1958) was a well-known psychical researcher associated with the ASPR, and a prolific author of parapsychology books. Ironically considering his role in the Crandon case, he was known for exposing fraudulent mediums.

The Meaning of Yourself

Once again, the pendulum had swung and in 1937 I started a revolt against my psychic work by writing a book entitled *My Life as a Search for Mediumship*[19], which contained a complete regurgitation of all the things that troubled me, predominantly: what was the meaning of life and the meaning of my mediumship? I made a tour of America saying farewell once again to psychic studies. I sensed that war was fast approaching and wanted to return to England in the Spring, which is what I did.

In Europe I embarked on a very merry, mad riot. Lucifer from time to time did cross my mind and with a smile I would consider: "Well, he *was* a very charming devil, but I really must have been a little mad to have thought of him!" I thought of him only in passing, but never sufficiently to attempt to bring him to me.

Then came the war, and my different attempts to get out of Fallen France; half-hearted attempts because I had the strong feeling that I must stay for an as yet undefined reason. I continued with work, but with no devil interruptions. During this time in the South of France, I became vitally interested again in the meaning of it all and in psychic research. I was one day, so to speak, struck as by lightning and challenged myself to find food for the displaced orphans. I knew then that I had a structure within a structure and that I must go and find out the meaning of it. With that in mind, I returned with difficulty to America.

When I arrived, I came to the conclusion that I must know America, and hence I entered the publishing arena. I realized I had a definition by which I could remember the orphan children's soup kitchen I worked with, and those orphans who wanted food and never could have it. They wanted to know when they would be fed. *Demain, cheris*, was the only answer to their

---

[19] Originally published in 1939; Afterworlds Press reprint 2022.

pleas for when food would come. "Tomorrow." Hence, I launched *Tomorrow Magazine*. The whole of America was talking in terms of despair and I was talking in terms of construction. For ten years I ran my publishing house, Creative Age Press, without ever thinking of my devil. Finally, regretfully, I had to give up my publishing endeavors due to ill health once again, resulting in three surgeries. I kept my severe medical problems from the members of my family and secretary, with them only realizing when I went into hospital that I was going in for something more than a cursory check-up.

I was very close to death. I didn't know what to do or where to turn. In desperation I called out to my "Noble Stranger," saying, "You know, if you were you and anywhere around, you would really know that I need you. Here I am in bed, and I need someone to talk with. Is this the time for you to pay a visit?"

I must have gone to sleep and when I woke up, he was there, looking very tired. He told me sharply "It's a very bad time to send for me, you know. It's a perdition—a time of perdition."

I laughed and said: "I presume you have your hands full."

He laughed and said: "My hands are very full."

I asked if he took it seriously?

"No, I don't take it seriously; men take it seriously."

I asked: "Is this all necessary?"

"Men think so—have thought so from the beginning of time."

"How will you cure them?"

"When the planet is finished, my work will be finished for a time."

"Oh!" said I. "Then where is my place?"

And he became exceedingly angry for the first time and said: "Get out of that bed! And get really busy. You have things to do. You have to know the meaning of yourself, and the meaning of life; now is the time to conceive of it."

So, I got out of my bed and in getting up started thinking of gathering together all the chiefs of psychic research to assess and share what they knew. This was really the beginning of my conceiving of what eventually became the Parapsychology

Foundation, which I established in 1951 as a worldwide forum supporting scientific exploration of psychic phenomena. I dedicated the rest of my life to its perpetuation.

We had parted company for a number of years and it was only at this point in my life that I asked him for help. Since that time, I would say that practically no day has passed that I don't salute him in my fashion or say "Hello, there," and very few nights have passed that I don't have long conversations with him.

The Hat and the Gown

Immediately after World War II was over, in looking over the situation I said to him: "I believe there are some 700 army divisions of men intact. What is going to happen to them?"

He said: "Don't worry. The country of your birth—your loyalty to Britain makes you understand of course that Britain has a great guilt—is already taking tenderly her German enemies to her bosom, as she's always done. And America, not quite so guilty but more foolish, will follow suit. And these people will be 'used' as all the officers are already training the Egyptian army. In a very short space of time they will weed England out of India, and then Egypt will follow suit, and the Sudanese will be taken as part of Egypt, and you will have a fine Arab rebellion."

He also told me: "Here your people are bothering about Russia. But nobody thinks of the wiser people, the Chinese who, twenty-five years from this day, will become such a terrible menace. Your country, your new country, is therefore like a doxy who thinks only in terms of her hat or her gown and whose underclothes are not given any thought. Take off the hat and the gown, and your new country will find itself bereft of decent underclothing. For this is where the menace lies."

Why Don't You Struggle with Me?

At this juncture of my life, I question Lucifer periodically and then, when I don't receive answers, I question God. Herewith is my struggle with God, my struggle to defend Him at times, my struggle to commit Him to my point of view, my struggle to "catch" Him, my struggle to accept Him, and finally my struggle to rebel against Him. Of all of this my companion is surely aware, and most certainly laughs at me, and says: "Why don't you struggle with me?"

I reply, "you have taught me not to struggle with you. You have taught me the meaning of temptation. You have taught me my way is not through you, but to Him."

He counters with "Why do you tempt Him with profanity? Why do you tell him he isn't? Why do you do all those things? What will you achieve?"

"I will burrow," I tell him "down below where you are to where He must be." And then I weep and wake up in tears as I struggle with the Infinite Intelligence, which sickens me in the struggle.

There is My Home

I suppose that my tantamount need for the "Noble Stranger" is obtaining the answers to my questions: "Just who are you? What is Heaven? What is God? What or who are these Guardians? Who are these Masters? Where are you in longitude and latitude? Are you under the waters or above? Where is your home?"

He turns my questions back on me and asks: "But where are you? Do you know? Aren't you between two oceans? Where is your longitude and latitude? Wherever you find yourself—a man finds himself—there is my home."

This gives me puzzlement, which requires a good deal of reflection. But most of my need of him—and it is undoubtedly a very egocentric need perhaps—is that I am concerned with my daily task, which is doing the right thing with and for people. I am concerned for the progress of my life in what I have always determined the right lines. But in my lifetime, with my peculiar gifts, I yearn to come in the door and pass out the gate knowing what happened. And so, my questioning is a very real need and desire in my heart to understand the meaning of God.

Now, God is a big word with which I wrestle, and I understand in my feelings all that it conveys: its Allness, its Wholeness. But the "Noble Stranger" is, in a sense, the only way by which I can reach that point, because the Other is too great, too altogether awesome. But that doesn't stop my worrying over the meaning of this shadow, shade, apparition, or as he calls himself, Lucifer.

In any case I find his sufferings deeper than any suffering, his compassion greater than any compassion, his understanding more definite that anything produced by the daily press. I find myself, you could say, somewhat always ahead of the game. Ego? Something I have produced of my own? This is why I like depth psychology—to find out what he is, who he is, and why I have such admiration for him.

Entourage of Spirits

I was excited at the beginning with him; I wondered about him, and wondered mostly about the state of my own mind that could conjure up something like him. At this time I was still worried about the nature of my controls, though I was somewhat certain that *he* was real. The thing that interested me was: "If I could conjure up this creature, why couldn't one of the controls come out and stand in Kensington High Street or Regent's Park or anywhere I was particularly happy and creative and have a talk with me—like my 'Noble Stranger' does?"

So, for a very long time, I was again really in doubt about my own sanity, in doubt as to whether he, or it, was what I thought as I named him: just a stranger. As a matter of fact,

I was very confused because I couldn't place this apparition in any particular place where it made any sense. That was one reason why I was quiet about him, not discussing him with many people, because I felt that if I added him to what I used to refer to as my "entourage" of supposed spirits, I would certainly have increased my difficulties in life.

I have regarded myself at times rather similar to a ham radio operator, picking up all these contacts, not knowing where they come from, very much as an amateur radio man never sees the face or knows very much about the personality of the message that he picks up from somewhere.

He gives me very great food for thought. If he could materialize and become three dimensional in a London busy street or in the canyons of New York, then prey tell what were my controls doing, *not* coming up to me to shake my hands and say "Well, how do you do, here we are, and stop worrying about us"?

A New Star Will Be Born

I do not understand why I am so reluctant to deal with my control personalities. They are quite aware of my reluctance. Many years ago when I was very ill, Uvani, who acts as the "Gatekeeper," was asked, "Why don't you look after your medium's health?" He said it was not the function of his coming. Dr. Abdul Latif, who is a known healer of body and soul, is always compassionate and yet I cannot in any sense understand my continued reluctance to be in some way intimate with them. I feel their job is to look after the world of people who need them through my mediumship and that I must necessarily look after myself.

I have always got the feeling, too, that perhaps it is not in the nature of me to be completely cured. Perhaps I bring upon myself many of these illnesses that plague me, because there is some point of ecstasy at which I do not know how to stop working, where I am caught in the action. I am a fairly practical, matter-of-fact individual, but I do catch myself from time to time producing the effects that are going to cause me later trouble and knock me down.

I wonder if these periods of illness, therefore, are lessons from which I learn a great deal about other people's illness? Are they matters and means by which I identify myself? Maybe so. I must know what each and every human being is talking about when he speaks of his illness.

The meaning of the controls lies deep somewhere in that closed room—awaiting somebody really sensible to understand them—as does the meaning of the "Noble Stranger." I have spoken to him about the health of the world, the health of the people. He responds to me, he laughs at me.

He tells me: "Cure them and they get into more difficulties."

I wonder if he is telling me something about myself that I don't quite realize. He will talk to me about many things, but he will not discuss my controls or their activities. He will not throw any light upon them whatsoever for me. He tells me that is my office. He will not talk to me about the health of the people. He rather cynically moves away.

I don't know much about Dr. Abdul Latif—only what has been told to Sir Arthur Conan Doyle, and of course about this I have my own personal reservations, because I must finally and every day ask myself why would two strange Oriental gentlemen be at my beck and call to answer the questions of the people. I ask it of Abdul Latif, and he says he answers the questions of all men, whether they have a pain in their toe, or a pain in their head, or a very great problem because he, too, in his way, is fond of people. Now, perhaps this is a reflection of myself because I, too, answer these questions, no matter how I am.

But what of the other gentleman who isn't in any sense hidden away? He's out in the open. Lucifer comes leisurely—not always when I want him, but he does eventually appear. He has talked about the process of the world of which I know nothing. He talks about the process of the planets. He tells me how the earth will one day be rushed into another flaming planet.

"Destruction?" I ask.

"Ah, no. Why does that word come to your mind? Of course not. The best of both will be kept. And the rest—they will amalgamate and a new star will be born. And the rest will fall upon the gentle territory below to again give life. Nothing is lost."

These are concepts that I've had for a long time. He has a wider aspect of knowledge. Sometimes I ask him, when I see a new drug on the market: "What is it?"

He names the compounds of it and says, "So what is that?"

My controls have no contact with me of this nature. They are always in their own longitude and latitude, whatever it may be. I believe that they are race memory, though wise philosophers tell me that there is no race memory. But wise philosophers have been known to change their minds. I still persist, until I get a better answer, that somewhere in the dramatic unconscious of this impatient youngster that was me, there must have come these dramatic splits and in walked these two archetypes, for want of a better word, on my father's side of the family as he was a Basque. As long as it gives me some peace of mind, I would prefer to think this way than contemplate the fact that these two—one who says he's not learned, and the other who pronounces his interest in learning—were individuals.

How can I believe that a simple country girl, born in Ireland, such as me, without any pretensions to anything but perhaps working on the farm, could suddenly find a couple of Oriental gentlemen hanging around in the atmosphere? It is much easier for me to deal with the devil—if devil he may be.

I do not see the controls, but I sometimes see the "Noble Stranger" out of the corner of my eye on occasion, but usually in front of me in three dimensions. He looks sometimes menacing, sometimes less menacing; sometimes very devilish, sometimes not so devilish, but always a lean, somewhat haggard and yet immensely calm and superior type of individual. He is accessible at all times, or nearly all times, and also doesn't "invade" me.

The Prince of Light

I have talked to him about sex; he's not interested. I have talked to him about food; he is not interested. I have asked him about hell, who made it up? And he tells me the theologians made it up. I asked him: "Does it exist?"

And he replied: "Yes, hell exists but mostly amongst the theologians." He is positively certain that the theologians are haunted by the concept of hell and that it becomes a very real necessity in their life.

I asked him: "do they believe in it?"

"No, not in the beginning of course. Finally they have talked about it so much that they are forever unsure."

I pursued my line of questioning again asking, "Does it exist in reality?"

And he replied: "Very much in reality."

"Does it have its territory?"

"In the heart of every man."

"Will it continue and be here a million years hence?"

"As long as there is the necessity for perfection...yes."

So his hell has, for my own peace of mind, become almost my own; at least he has given me a very interesting concept of hell. But he has been equally amusing about heaven. Many years ago, I asked him: "Now about this place where people wish to go because they are good...?"

He seized on the word "good" and said: "But what is goodness?"

Then we had a long discussion about doing the best one knows in life, which is also something that I use very often in my own life and which I got from him.

And then he sketched a scene of this heaven, saying: "Now just imagine yourself being received by this pontifical soul saying 'You may enter here.' And in your concept you enter into a green and lovely garden, and you are handed a combination of clothing, entirely unbecoming to your shape. And then you are given a musical instrument, one rather like that in your native land, though I believe more Grecian in type, and you are asked to strum upon it for the rest of your life. So, it boils down then that your Christian theology has taught you that you enter into this glorious state of calm and tranquility, where you will wear this clothing, you fly around, and you perpetually spend your time playing upon an obscure musical instrument."

He added: "May I politely suggest to you that this indeed, for you, would be a variation of hell infinitely worse than any hell that I, the Prince of Darkness, could conceive of. Incidentally, I am not the Prince of Darkness but of Light."

He pricks holes in all the biblical stories from the very beginning of Genesis, and he shows how really futile they are in the light of modern civilization and science. I ask him about the great Prophets and the great Masters, and he will say to me: "Take care that some of the dust doesn't rub off on your own shoulders."

Another thing that he saved me from, inasmuch as he made me very conscious of it, was the fact that people are always gathering together in the name of somebody; they want to lionize you or even deify you, as they did Mary Baker Eddy, the faith healer. And he always warned me: "Beware when you see people wanting to sit at your feet, because this will be the death of your inspiration, and it will be the death of your ambition to understand; because if you would seek understanding for yourself, then, of course, you would only be inhibited by such people. And it is not in any case your role in life." Then he laughs and says: "Get someone to ask your friends and they will tell you it is not your role in life." He refers to the control personalities always as "my friends" in a rather cool manner.

I confess that he laughs at me a great deal. He is sometimes kindly, when I insist on hearing a thing two or three times. When I ask him about the Temptation, the days of Gethsemane, he says: "No, I wasn't there. He was by himself. He didn't need my presence. It was enough that he had withdrawn..."

But; "Oh yes," he once countered, "of course I was there."

He has done one other thing for me. By virtue of pointing out to me the pitfalls and faults of the whole essence of theology, he has given me my own understanding of life. By pointing out to me the meaning of desire, he has freed me from it. I have said to him: "but my life is passing by and I permit the sexual side of my life to pass away from me. What do you think of that?"

He answered: "What would it be now but repetition, what is there left? You're not creating that illusion for yourself any longer."

Perhaps he has made himself so superior to any intelligence, any male intelligence that I would seek, that he has even taken away desire. My friend Lucifer has really left me completely desireless, because there is nothing like him on earth, and certainly not in heaven. If I would ask him about any of the things a human being must deal with in relationships, he would walk away. He is only interested in what he calls the intellectual spreading of the carpet before my eyes so that I may not fill myself with illusions, and consequently hamper my search for meaning.

His main purpose in my life seems to be the purpose that was fulfilled when I was a youngster by the great revolutionaries in Ireland, by these men who were always talking Home Rule and who saw the great carpet of the world at their feet: the world they were going to conquer.

He has no liking for anybody in Russia particularly, yet he does not individualize any of them. But when I ask him of our elder statesmen here in America, he does say: "They are very useful indeed—because you see, the very thing that they are talking about is the thing that has already taken hold of them." He referred once to John Foster Dulles[20] as a man "swimming in water but held in the arms of a gentle octopus."

---

[20] A United States Republican politician and diplomat who served as Secretary of State under Dwight D. Eisenhower, 1953-59. He was known for his aggressively anti-communist stance and advocating the Cold War U.S. military buildup.

Happiness is a State of Sadness

He tells me that one day he will regain the Kingdom of Strength. He says: "When this planet's work is finished, I will regain the kingdom of strength."

"To be happy?" I question.

He responds "But happiness is a state of sadness. It is a desert. And it cannot last for long in man's mind. It is only a little place for introspection, and no place to dwell for long, because in happiness there is no growth."

When I try to speak to him of God, he shrugs his shoulders and speaks of the Giver of Strength; the Giver of Life; the Giver of Light. If I ask him: "Am I profane in my attitude toward the Deity?" he shrugs his shoulders.

I tell him: "One of these days I am going to kick over the traces and I am going to do this and I am going to do that."

He then comments: "Well, that would be a return to ignorance."

"To innocence?" I query.

"No man is innocent once he has turned his eyes to the stars and asks questions."

He seems interested in my search for the truth: he demands it, he prods me and he pries open little aspects in my own character. He is pitiless at times—but completely agreeable.

I never call him "devil." He himself declared: "Call me Lucifer," and I have no other reason. I have, of course, been told by many theologians that I am in fact speaking to the devil, to which I can only say that I have learnt so much more from him about theology and the ways of Christian ethics, and certainly the ways of the Roman and Hebrew ethics, and the ways of the Prophets, than I could have learned from any theologian directly or through any writings. I also see the panorama of the world, spread out with new ideas shaping and changing the world through my interaction with him.

Once I asked him: "Now the Pope is a very learned man. Does he think as you think?"

"I beg your pardon?"

I again asked, "but does he think as you think?"

"But it is not possible for him to think, because, if he were to think, he would become 'ander'[21] and to be 'ander' he would not be glorified, and consequently he may not think." With that he looks up and says: "But he only ever thought one way."

I ask, "What is that way?"

"Read his history and you will find out."

"But he serves your purpose," I said.

"Admirably. He sets up new formulas at all times. The more formulas you set up, the more you entangle your mind."

As I considered this I asked: "Therefore, all the formulas that he has set up about the matriarchal mother, are they correct?"

"Well, everything is correct in theory, but in practice it does no good."

I once asked him: "Why did he send Mary to heaven?"

And he told me: "In order to capture Wall Street." And he went his way.

Abstractions and Distractions

When I speak of my "Noble Stranger" who calls himself "Lucifer" I also think of Venus, the morning star, the brightest object in the sky after the sun and moon. The Rebel Angel also comes to mind, whose pride brought his fall. To me, he is, in any case a being. Perhaps because I have met him during my experience with LSD 25, I comprehend "him" for what he may mean for me. He is not light or luciferous, since until I took LSD I had

---

[21] The word "ander" has various meanings in different European languages, though perhaps the Indo-European root "under" or "second" is meant here, in the sense that if the pope were to think beyond Catholic dogma, he would not remain head of the Church for long. The Old English "submissive" or "dominated" would make similar sense.

not particularly thought of him as a creature of darkness. The name Luce is Light, and *ferre* is to bring him out of darkness; yet unconsciously I set the scene for a realistic meaning with this entity in my room, where I close myself in the darkness of night.

In my unconscious reasoning, I think of "him" as an entity of moral and intellectual significance, a "phosphorescent" one perhaps, made more luminous against the darkness of the night. I do not think I ever attached "evil" motivations to his presence, nor associations embodying any of the accepted knowledge of him, whether sacred or profane. I have no real knowledge of evil; perhaps I think of it as anything that can cause malicious harm to others. I regard sin in much the same way, or as a process of evolution: something that develops from a pre-existing form, which must be as one experiences exfoliation, as does the mineral world, the plant or tree, by change through experience.

In this way, I think of the "Noble Stranger" not as the Devil or vicious, but as being rather knavish, clever perhaps, mischievously energetic on behalf of growth within the self: a superhuman, magnificent creature. That he could devise, plot, plan or scheme to affect one's will toward experience, I have no doubt; nor would he care which way the experience led. Perhaps his work is one of devolution. One has to be thrown against life, to fall, to be tempted, before one can investigate the self and deal with all its metaphysical conclusions and solutions.

For me, our conversations have been a harmonious melody: a range of ideas, perhaps foundation notes in the symphony of life. Now it has become an opaque melody better remembered, no longer diatonic, for the master of the melody has not given me revelation since I took LSD and extended my inner vision of his probable meaning for me.

I know that the "image" of my "Noble Stranger" has great knowledge of human frailties. He knows suffering deeper than one can describe. His understanding of the depths of the deep unconscious was revealed when men, during the Jewish

Terror[22], killed each other without real understanding of the price which would one day have to be paid, when Pride again and again must be humbled by other forces.

I feel he offers resistance to love and compassion, as though love would enslave him. Yet I once asked him if love didn't rule the world?

He thought a while and said: "Yes, for a brief moment of innocence, or illusion, but," he asked, "What of sensuality? Will it not take over Cardinal, statesman, and lover? Besides, one could not dwell in bliss for too long a season. The barbarians of nature take over to destroy man's ethics, for Love is not a substance that can endure; it is, at best, a 'technique,' make no mistake. In the innocent heart of the babe, passion, wrong, and anger sleep side by side behind the sculptured innocence; valor and fear are blood brothers."

Once he laughed wryly and said: "All your compassions are like your gods, abstractions and distractions."

"Yes," I answered, "but no illusions either."

Two Rivers Flowing Toward Eternity

I once asked him to tell me something about Eleusis. His answer was most descriptive. Eleusis, apparently, was once a village, or perhaps for want of a better description a series of small towns of which Eleusis itself was the largest. Its people were old in sorcery, old in intrigues. There were many reasons why they were able to protect themselves from being invaded or mixed with other tribes. A prominent hill commanded a full view of the sea. Here lived the king of the group, for there were as many kings as townships, and all lived behind dense fortifications. With plains east and north of them, they had access from their high bastions, but each small town adjoining

---

[22] This is presumably a reference to the Holocaust, though could also refer to the persecution of Jews throughout the centuries.

was also fortified. The slopes and fortifications were protected by an all-enveloping exterior wall. This was at a time of great scarcity of water, which made the many cisterns and wells not only sacred, but something to be guarded, nay treasured, for man and flocks alike. The river Kephinos clearly flowed at the foot of the hills, for the high mountains of Parnassus and Cithaeron, which shut the plain within from attack, also providing streams. Even today, when nothing is left behind but stories from the past and ruins, water still flows, but far below.

The Goddess Demeter came to Eleusis and had her quarrel with mighty Zeus within the cavern walls of the cave of Pluto.

I asked: "Did Demeter know Olympia?"

"Yes, and like all interfering women who do malice with too little knowledge and too much curiosity, she was expelled from the city and came to Eleusis."

"But" I asked him, "they were real, these women, or just names from other elements?"

"Oh yes," he answered, "real enough. Wasn't Mary, the Mother of your Lord, real? Haven't you after several centuries made her a dominant force for your own good purposes?"

"Did Demeter have knowledge extraordinary?"

"All goddesses have guile, are purposeful, some of them subtle enough to form their ends, all of them interested to misgovern and rule mankind."

"Why then do men worship them?"

"Because they are the principle of life, the Mother of life, the Incubator of the child. Their relationship to the elements of life cannot be denied nor suppressed. They long to govern that which they worship."

"You must find them useful?"

"But yes," he answered. "Tools of the elements always, but like tools they must be kept sharpened, bright and cleansed of the grime with which they employ their time."

"Where did the Goddess Demeter come from?"

He answered: "Driven from Olympia, she came to the plains, to the seat of the King of Eleusis. She was a sorceress."

"What was her cult, which lasted for one thousand years?"

"She passed on through centuries the rites performed to ensure crops, cattle, children, foods, and powers. There were as many 'Demeters' as there are 'wise women' all over the world. In Catholic countries, they all can be gathered under the goddess Mary, whose cult has lasted a few centuries also. The Christian Church replaced Demeter and all her followers by appointing Mary on the same date, August 15th, as the Mother of God when she passed into the Heavens as so designed by dogma. There is no difference, only the names have changed."

"Where do the Eleusinians come from?"

"Out of Asia Minor, as indeed did the forerunners of the Greeks. The Athenians took over the rule of the Eleusinians and made them their own to officially recognize them under the guise of worship!"

"What has made Eleusis memorable?"

"It owed its glory to being a city of mysteries and the sanctuary of Demeter."

"Was she wise?"

"Today your theologians would raise their brows over cannibalism, even though some of your churches preach it in mystic form! The beginning of your 'body blood' idea was hers also, as it was also the custom of all the early agricultural 'goddesses' to use sometimes their first born, often their first lovers, or husbands if you like the term better, and at the end of the year shed his blood; his bones to furnish the earth while the other members of the household, mostly guards, ate his heart, their seat of the emotions and the soul. The priests preserved the entrails for clairvoyance."

"What was so horrible, only the customs?" I asked him.

"Nothing terrible in nature, but the mysteries all had to do with sex, blood sacrifice, death, and all the rituals that belong. In a sense, these things viewed in their right perspective were in order for their time. Men believed in the Gods, and the imagination of the Goddesses was always turned toward lust and the conservation of life and the consecration of the Earth.

But these ceremonies, however innocent they may have been, can through the centuries become obscene. Men and women alike worship at the obscene altars more readily than in the plain air before a growing tree."

"But," I asked, "then as today, trees were worshipped?"

"Yes," he told me, "and the blood of many smeared them to make the worship more powerful, the magic more convincing."

"What was the temple of Demeter like?" I asked him.

"An ordinary dwelling house as used by people of the times, wherein dwelt the Goddess, withdrawn toward an inner room, such as one sees today in the country where a few flowers and icons form a place for worship. Her inner closet or storehouse, buried deep in the forest, contained all the material and salves by which she healed or made her charms. Yes, they worked, since the cult continued for several hundred years, but," he added maliciously, "so does the Christian cult. One day men will stand before the high altars of Christendom and ask of each other: 'What did they believe?' It was ever thus."

"Does Christian magic work?" I asked.

"Yes, for some."

"But in very remote days, was magic powerful?"

"Yes," he answered, "because men believed it."

"Is there anything left of the early shrines?"

"Yes, the earth. Each new goddess of Demeter had to have her new temple or an addition, her servitors their new administrative buildings."

"Would you say then that Eleusis was recognized as being always a sacred edifice?"

"Yes, so is St. Peter's in Rome. I see no difference, only in ritual."

"What has started Satan worship?"

"Man's deep desire to rule the Universe and have it obey him alone."

"Does it obey him?" I asked.

"Seemingly so," he answered, "to burn his fingers and finally destroy him. In older days, as in the days of your Eleusinian goddesses, food and drink were the potent purveyors by which magic was arranged."

"Yes," I answered, "that must have led to poison...."

"According to the potency, precisely. Men have always separated forever from the beginning."

"Why?" I asked him.

"Because," he answered, "they are themselves two rivers flowing toward eternity—one placidly flowing, and the other turbulently."

"Which are you?" I asked him.

"Oh," he answered flippantly, "both of course—how you prattle...."

Beauty and the Beast of Light

Much later I reopened our conversation and asked: "You are, because man is?"

He explained: "Yes! I am the constant, persistent suggestion that makes for creation. I am not really passive, only as it suits the role; the myths of the first man contain one, just as does the ever-inexhaustible energy of the Cosmos pour forth its experience. I am its guiding law. Without me it cannot grow. Religion, myth, art, yes even science, technology, all—all that man conceived of to blister him, days and nights, must arise from his demand for power, for these dreams must prove to goad man onward. Man being in a state of swollen unshapeliness cannot live without the dream that, pure when it arrives, is beaten by him to serve him. The continued love story and tragedy of living must go on! Call it Beauty and the Beast: love, passion, adoration, whatever. Man's impulses drive him to become at once both beauty and beast. But the cruel, ignoble, magical, theological—what are words—they only make more trouble. I am that which I am, that the word shall prove."

"But once you were the Beast of Light, how then did you become Satan?"

He did not deign to answer.

Like the Rest of the Elements

"What were some of the exact methods used at Eleusis?" I asked one day.

"They were largely concerned with producing elements of the Gods—their voices mostly, but sometimes as in latter day lore, the priests assumed their supposed shape and vestments. Most of the rituals are contained in all forms of magic, among which fear of possession by demons and the dead demanded fearsome rituals to impress the people. Many of the rituals have passed into the Semitic languages and were practiced by the Semites. Much of the Powezne[23] rituals were concerned with demanding powers from the powerful angels, for theology had not arrived to create me."

"But, for all man's life through uncounted centuries, you were there?"

"Yes, like the rest of the elements that serve to shape the universe. I was there; but in many guises, as I have explained, because the force of the hammer that beats out the iron on the Anvil of Life must be strong, as must the anvil to withstand the shock of the hammer blows."

"Then it is the clerical monks preaching against other gods, spells, etc.—witchcraft in other words—" I added slyly, "that created you?"

"Yes," he sighed, "the bad powers in your theological circles have adopted me and, shall we say, served me well, but warned the simpletons against me."

---

[23] What exactly is meant by "Powezne" is obscure. It is unclear if it is supposed to be a specific kind of ritual, or if it is meant to denote the rituals of a certain Semitic people. In either case, there is no known relevant association. In Polish, "powezne" means "serious" though that hardly makes sense in the context.

"Have men always worshipped you?"

"Yes, but not always under this pseudonym. You should ask your Arab controls about me—they were for a time deeply involved in magic, but perhaps those were more ancient than your own."

"When you were not Satan or the Devil, what then?"

"Oh, always a genii of one type or another. I have as many names as there are stars visible. For once the stars themselves were the bringers of bad fortune."

"But always men regarded you as being related to Celestial Intelligence?"

"This, yes," he answered and left me hurriedly. Now I wonder if it was something that I had said that caused him to end our conversation.

The Blood of Life

Through my further study of Eleusis[24] I came to comprehend that a total understanding of the rites was impossible, for the best guides had been inhibited from divulging anything that took place within, on pain of death. The "mystia," or those who took part in the rites, were chosen by the priests of Demeter. Usually they gathered together in the inner court of the temple, near the spring, to perform rites of purification. Many of the rites involved the scourging of the body, and the Flagellantes

---

[24] It is unclear if she means "study" via Lucifer or through her own reading, though it should be noted that much of what is written in these sections conflicts with what is known of Eleusis and its Mysteries in traditional Classical scholarship—especially the more sensational claims such as flagellation, sex orgies, human sacrifice, and bestiality. For an introductory overview, see Hugh Bowden (2010) *Mystery Cults of the Ancient World*. Princeton: Princeton University Press. For a short but more scholarly work, see Walter Burkert (1987) *Ancient Mystery Cults*. Cambridge, Mass: Harvard University Press.

were born of these rites. The procession, from the towns around, of the dignitaries who came to observe and applaud before the sacred gates, were watched in awe by the common people who felt that some of the magic of the priestess Demeter/Kore must rub off on the dignitaries and so, perhaps, onto them. These processions became awesome in consequence. They may even have functioned within the numerous temples that grew up in the worship of the Gods who looked on with satisfaction, but the sacred way was trodden upon only by the feet of those whose blood would be offered in sacrifice. Many sacrifices of animals were necessary along the way, by those who would then offer themselves as sacrifices. For them there were many large quadrangles, each containing an altar and a permanent grate to hold the sacred water, for these sacrifices were made to the gods of the elements and their wives—Zeus ruling over all!

After the Greeks, the Romans took over and added considerably to the number of buildings so that, while the magic of Demeter and Kore continued, other gods were introduced. Palaces and buildings were akin to the monasteries of the Middle Ages in Europe. We, however, must confine ourselves to the early agricultural rites dedicated to the gods who, man felt, dwelled behind the elements: the sun, moon, and stars, as well as air and water, and the turbulence of the elements themselves.

The Noble Stranger explained to me: "We go back, therefore, to the time long before Solon[25], and think of the sacred place as the ancients conceived of it. We will forget the crowds, the dignitaries, the priests and rich ones who came for the spectacle and to consult the sacred mother, and we will confine ourselves to the mysteries of the telesterion where the magic and mysterious rites took place. It was a large square room with stone steps, which led down to the sunken floor on all four sides. The telesterion was 'received' in plan and design from the Gods themselves. The floor was at a depth of 25 feet,

---

[25] Athenian poet and politician, 630-560 BCE.

the roof opened, much as can be observed in early Byzantine churches—open to the blessing, dismay, or joy of the Gods.

"In the north part of the room were the vestments in a sealed cubicle, and on the other side of the cubicle of the vestments were the boxes of oak which contained relics and sacred objects used at the ceremonies, as well as the sacred torches. The mysteries were of such a nature that all the symbolism contained in sacred draughts—cleansings with functioning and mal-functioning—were intended to prepare those selected by the earth mother to make their peregrination in another world. Therefore, the sensualities were necessary to cleanse the body and mind before entering the habitation of the Gods."

"The sensualities," I asked him, "were what?"

"Often the flesh was castigated and when bleeding was profuse, herbs and their juices were rubbed into the wounds, which stimulated the body to suffer more torture so that the mind escaped to the Eleusian fields. The painful, wearisome wandering of Demeter in search of her daughter became a part of the theater in which the priests and novices alike took part. The choir sang mournfully the cries of Demeter for 'the daughter found and restored,' as one spectacle ended to make way to another. A young prince arrived before the goddess for his crowning, his carriage drawn by slaves, in his left hand the scepter of his royal rank, in his right, ears of corn. There would be before his crowning many peregrinations of a mystical nature to take place, so that he may personally speak with the Gods and define his rank, because for one year he will be the husband of Demeter. It will be for him later to choose one who will follow him, for at the year's end he will be sacrificed here, as will he who was her husband. Their blood will be given to the earth; their flesh and entrails, with much magic, will be conveyed to the trees and plants who will give back full blooming. The ancients believed that the most priceless thing was the blood of life. Therefore, if one would find satisfaction with the Gods, one must give the blood to the earth, if the earth would produce."

Here the "Stranger" averted his face and murmured: "The earth continues to be a greedy mother: witness the blood of sacrifice that men unworthily offer each day to her needs. Only now the magic and mystical need has been replaced..."

"By what?" I asked him.

"Greed," he answered, "Diabolical greed."

Where Lies the Difference?

"Were there other oracles present?"

"Yes, the then world abounded with them, each reading the signs according to his temperament. Mostly the symbols were concerned with the flight of birds (messengers), an unusual plumage and a donation from the gods. The questions? The same as today. Man, always unsure as to his own meaning, sought by all routes to understand the meaning of himself! Those versed in the power to perceive carried the destiny of trade, armies, navies, kings and their subjects!"

"Were the oracles forged?"

"Even as today! Yes, by politicians, chiefs and all who held power over the peoples."

"Then," I asked, "the city or state and the oracle collaborated?"

"Yes, why not?"

"May we speak again of the Eleusinian sanctuary?"

"Yes, if you will, it was the Vatican of its day—why not? After all, it was the Christian religion that finally destroyed the buildings to make their own religion no less useful, no more important."

"Were all men permitted to Eleusis? For I must bear in mind that there were slaves."

"Yes, men, women and children. The sanctuary was revered by all. The presence of all became necessary for the religion of the people. The dedication of the slaves and deification of the children, all sprang from Eleusis."

"Would you say that the Mass and Catholic teaching was left over?"

"No, Catholic teaching is a form of Neo-Judaism that is the outgrowth of the Semitic god Yahveh. Only the pomp and the singing bears relation. Many gods were worshipped at Eleusis. Man came by sea from Asia Minor, in waves and surges, to learn at the Sanctuary."

"Then in a way, it was like modern Rome, this Eleusis?"

"Yes, and equally decadent; you must consider Catholicism decadent."

"What of the Protestant religions? There are so many."

"I see no difference. A man wants wives—he protests—again a religion is born! Lutheranism? Calvinism? Republicanism? Nihilism? Communism? Where lies the difference? Power in the name of God. But power in the hands of the few over the many. This is not religion!"

"Was Eleusis, perhaps in the beginning, religion? At least they believed that what they offered had meaning to the Gods."

"The mysteries were of course related to the growth of the land. There were then two periods: the spring blooming, and the departing of the heat from the earth, or autumn, as you call it now: Life and Death. All children of the powerful had to be initiated into the mystery of Life and Death, and all the children were catechized even as in your churches. The emphasis was on making the body clean, pure, strong, and noble. The training for children was severe. The training for the active mysteries the most severe, for then one identified oneself with the mystery of death, and had to be strong to fortify against it, and yet to compete to accept it with stoicism."

"Would you say that the emphasis on training was what we call today sex lore?"

"Yes certainly. Men and more men had to be produced! The earth demanded them. More and more children had to be brought into the world. The training, very severe in both cases, had most emphasis on bodybuilding, but with solemnity. The sacred mysteries were never touched by the ordinary women, only the priests and the priestesses; they had to be carried long distances to outlying countries where the people fell in the dust and worshipped them. Much chanting, many processions took place. A month of days was devoted to this, each day a different devotion. But out of this month, nine days were always devoted to purification."

"Did that include total abstinence?"

"On the contrary! The mind was emptied of carnal imaginings by a surfeit of sex orgies so that every part of the body functioning was brought into relief. Then, and only when the carnal man was dissipated, could the spiritual man take over in preparation for the great mysteries of the mind and spirit. Offerings were made to the God of the Sea during this time of purification, and many small animals were sacrificed at this time. Children: deformed, crippled, or otherwise unable to take the force of life, became sacrifices to the elements, to the sea gods. It was a way of strengthening the race.

"The great mysteries of copulation with gods who took the form of animals and grotesque men were accomplished on the last two days, in almost total darkness. Oracles went forth looking for the unusual that the gods might make of them vessels. Grief, joy, fear, then finally abandon and exultation followed. The initiates who lived through the experience of copulation with all that was brought within the mystia survived and believed that henceforth they were new and better men because their souls had entered into unhallowed liaison with nature. Now, their souls saved, their happiness after death was assured. No one could tell of what happened on those two mysterious nights, for in truth, none within the darkness, their senses sharpened and intoxicated, could really describe their feelings, nor admit one to the other their intoxication or abandon. The rape of Kore by Pluto and the rape of mortals by Gods in various forms, accompanied by sacred stories and various objects of the several cults, were of course first played as a great spectacle for the initiates; these roles were held by actors who played out the divine drama before the initiation commenced.

"For those who ever tried to reveal the mysteries of the initiation, there was instant death. No man could reveal the ritual without meeting death; for those who attempted to speak out, or parody the mysteries, death was unavoidable. Thus, silence by fear of death in a most horrible fashion kept the mysteries from being understood."

The Ultimate Destruction

"There is no doubt that there was a strong mingling of cults in Eleusis. Many priests and their oracles came to what was the governing site of religious experience. Many go to Rome today to make their pilgrimage and seek blessing. Their orders and vestments, as well as their rank, makes for difference in their method of service, but surely the basis of order is dictated from Rome. Thus it was with Eleusis. There were extensive trade routes between the Asian and African countries, while the need for and use of slaves kept profitable wars going, and raids on each other's territory were as commonplace as they are today."

"Today?" I enquired.

"Do not allow me to imagine that you think your statesman and priests do not have their hands covered with the blood of sacrifice. They are more careful to hide the ways and means today, and do not refer to the Gods needing as much attention."

"There was no purity in the hearts of men, then or ever?"

"Yes, in the hearts of the few, but then they were enlightened enough to keep their standards from the mass of the people, or they would too fall into disrepute."

"Yet Eleusis stood for centuries before Greece even?"

"You mean Athens perhaps? Greece is like the Commonwealth and the Arab states, made up of blood kingship into which poured the lesser states and their slaves. It is true that each blended into the common need. Slaves brought more than their bodies, they brought their methods of religion; spies accompanied them and beautiful young creatures were sent, too, to weaken the hearts of ruler and priestess alike. The very nature of worship demanded more show and striving after power, as man seized his brother's power together with his slave, for flesh of slave nature went at high price, as each ruler and each priestess bethought themselves of new palaces and new ways to assuage their senses."

"Were the oracles drugged?"

"Certainly the young were, while the older ones grew well to obey the demand of the ruling powers and 'foretell' accordingly. You ask about the services and their mystical nature. Undoubtedly, they had some purity to commence with, for man faced with death is often awed; thus to the elements he prayed for his life and its sustenance, and made them his Gods, but finally the Gods took second place when man no longer feared. It was thus and it must always be. But the people, then as now, needed to hear the voice of the Gods who cannot always be commanded. There were those trained to speak for them."

"The mysteries?" I asked.

"Oh those," he laughed. "Take any parade of men's emotions, dress it to evoke admiration and awe, mix it with love, play, sports and athletic games, pleasure with animals alleged to sometimes play out the drama for the Gods. Then sweeten the rest with purges, fasting, purification and dedication to any particular spirit, or dream, or power drive; mix well your potencies with blood and wine, and mix the body seed of the blood of young men and maidens; light your torches and prepare your sacred flames, thus inflame the minds of those who know too well, and the minds of those who would know. Bring out the young, the tender and the meek; dress them with garlands and flowers; bring on your music and feast; address to your priests all that their hearts desire; sing songs, strum the lyres of a thousand melodies in strange voice, and prepare in darkness such erotic fantasies as the heart wills, and you can—with enough sacrifice and reason for making same—have your mystery. Add to all this the sexual demands and blood lust under cover of darkness and secrecy, and you will find the rich, the powerful and the jaded will give lavishly."

"If this were all, why has nothing been preserved in the history of Eleusis?" I asked.

"This is easy. Be certain that these things are given only to the most powerful, but keep well their names before you for that day that they would seek power, so that you have a whip with which to control them. Also, there are more slaves in the world than powerful ones; if you want to keep them in subjection, keep them always believing in the 'absolute' of the few. This the people demand. Thus there will always be the undiminished supply of slaves. To do this well, keep your battlefields fresh and crown the victors."

"You are so cynical! People today are tired of wars."

"Now," he remarked, "you wax foolish and sentimental. Did your recent wars demand sacrifice? Does the policy of using the energy of the planet to build fires to send objects whirling into space, to burn the crops of the earth and the very earth itself, even the breath of earth, smell of man's weariness with evil? I tell you, man today is more wretchedly craven, more wholly dissolute and more cruel in his ways to punish his brother than he has ever been. He is also without respect or reverence for himself, and this, more than his lusts, is the ultimate destruction."

The First Word

"Tell me Lucifer, did men in other days believe in their Gods?"

"There have always been the serfs and slaves who had to believe that somewhere, on some day, by the power of some God, they might see hope and rest. But on the whole, once man achieved a little knowledge of his surroundings, he became himself 'the God and the Image.' I would say that man's belief is like the earth's borning. When the soul is dark, he tends to look beyond, but when the room of the soul is well furnished and lighted, he is content with his own majesty."

"Do you believe, then, that the priests and Goddesses alike wielded their power knowingly?"

"But yes. Always. They may have been in awe to begin with, and all too soon they usurp the powers for themselves."

"But there were always holy men of nobility, and those who like myself are wrapped in a deep faith."

"Yes," he agreed, "Alas, always the small minority. This, too, has always been."

"Who were the first Gods?" I demanded.

"Birds," he answered. "They even now continue to be messengers of good or evil. And then, the animals who had strength beyond human's notion. Also the snake because of its phallic interpretation, for the phallus was, of course, worshipped as the key to life in all countries and at all times, in all seasons. Small animals that dig below the ground had their uses, too, to guide man's nostrils toward the changing seasons; but the large animals and the birds were invariably the messengers and the seat of the Gods. The woman, bearer and giver of life, was easily promoted to goddess-ship before men realized that their own participation in sexual ritual produced children. No animal knows what he does in rut. For long centuries, therefore, woman was as the torch-bearer who led the way toward perpetual continuity because of the fruit of her womb. She brought forth life and so blessed the earth from her womb with the children who would follow to care for the earth. Consequently, the trees, fruit of the earth, and plants, gave of their being, also to feed, to clothe and to bring changes of temperature to man. Trees were at one time the rightful dwelling place of the Gods."

"Is there much change in religious practice today?"

"I do not find your 'lip service' exacting, nor your religion of any account. It is a pantomime through which many pass in ritual form as of yore, but few are touched to understanding. You still have your idols and your Earth Mother, but they are in almost all lives well removed from usefulness. Belief in either power of 'good' or 'not good' is no longer belief. Because of this lack within, man is no longer able to reach his better self, and for lack of nourishment, perishes."

"And you?" I asked.

"I shall continue," he replied.

"As what?" I asked him.

"Perpetual change," he answered, "neither good nor yet evil; neither God nor Demon."

"But–" I began to question.

"Excuse me," he said sharply. "I told you long ago. Call me Lucifer if you must—He Who Brings Light, and Light was, according to the ancients, the first word."

The Vital Source

Once, when staying in Florida, I had gone to the beach and entered the cabana where one lazed in the nude and took a sun bath, and at the same time was deeply engrossed in a book. Suddenly, I was not alone: the "Noble Stranger" arrived. I made hasty apologies for being in a state of undress. It mattered little to him.

"I believe you are ruining your skin by lying in the strong sunlight, and furthermore, the sun saps your energy on all levels. A little is good but the body will rebel. You have a weak heart and lungs that have been, from time to time, troublesome. Do not waste time laying up troubles for yourself for, while the sun is the life giver, he can also be an enemy. Why do you not go into the shade and write from your Celtic Heavenworld?"

I reflected for a moment and then answered: "I can only write while I am in the mood; today, I have nothing to say."

"You have been a listener for a long time; why not disgorge some of these 'essays'?"

"One may not do that," I told him. "I regard my work as the priest does."

"There are only so many conflicts in the world of man–"

I interrupted by reminding him: "You sound more like a guru today."

"There are many methods of teaching," he replied; "no metaphors or citations are necessary—originality is the way of your Western world. Knowledge is important but it must be spontaneous and does not arise from a wandering mind.

"Identify yourself with the vital source of life itself, and you will note that the external forces compel you to be spontaneous."

Embodied in One and All

For me, the experience of looking into the subconscious aspects of the self has been highly revealing. I feel that there has been an understanding on many levels: a discipline of cleansing to let memory bring forth other aspects of self. Even now, though I have still got much preserved within that flash of insight, I feel there is much more to be revealed. There are other experiences in the nature of self to arise and be understood.

I have asked myself what the revolutionary within life really means—religious, philosophic, or driven, as he often is, by power. What is the power that guides each one toward eventual extinction?

Some significant fragments of one of my most recent conversations with the "Noble Stranger" have fallen into place and should be considered. He shared with me:

"There is a sensitivity within, equally beautiful as the poets, which may be, as was the case of Hitler, affected by unsympathetic criticism. The man possessed by imagination has to go deeper within, not to be sensitive to criticism, or he will become sour and withdrawn, unable to sense the discipline which criticism bestows, and so he may be given an opportunity to impose his will on others. Of course, there will always be those who affirm superiority in mediocrity. Their 'understanding' can become immediately identified by the person as a 'cause,' until the humble exercise of faith in oneself becomes extinct. Many failures in leadership have thus occurred—none more easily than the support of those who, for their own ends to be served, become followers."

The Noble Stranger once assured me "All men have the truth within themselves. The divine is embodied in one and all."

Dogmas, their uses and abuses have always intrigued me, so I raised that topic often. He told me, "The two principles of growth and progress must continue, bound as it were, by a ligature. Both elements are, of course, lapped by the winds of will and desire within each person."

Lucifer went on to opine: "The excited mind may have difficulty at first in choosing to clarify the creative attention. The need for self-expression can be dominated by the need for self-importance, rather than the importance of self, until the original motivation bogs down, and the original creative intention gets blurred. The submission to self will take over domination, and the personal body and ego will then emerge to make other powerful strides rebuffing the serenity of wisdom. Once this happens, the imagination can easily be manipulated by those others who seek power. Impressions no longer arising from the serene will are now conveyed by the 'implicators.' Thus does harmony of self and morality become dim, to be given negative postulates. Experience, once dimmed by this new field of experience, produces drama, which, in turn, produces conflict and rules out that inner valuable introspection where goodness once reigned. Man soon learns to do the will of his priests and advisers, his generals and his guards, so that the pure creative recognition is lost, as well as man's secret identity. Man has always shrunk from the fire of his own spiritual serenity, to give way before the supreme egoism, which finally destroys the modest seal of devotion.

"The power of human thinking longs to give shape to a new interpretation of God, and in times of stress or difficulty, people are apt to proclaim their need. How often in man's history the people's need has demanded new insight, but their masters and guides, not wishful of having their power diminished, rob them again and again of the fruits of their imagination and courage?"

The Key to All that Exists

The years have passed easily. Now in the late 1960s, my daughter is at my desk in the office; my grandchildren are serious; they respect my vocation and rarely dwell on it. Perhaps my continual arthritis slows down the pace of living and also my external interests. The experience, however, of interacting with Lucifer, my "Noble Stranger," continues unabated.

I now wonder sometimes if he is a collective image of illumination handed down through the ages. Through the vast number of years, the word among the "do nots" has been that given to the strength of the devil. As far as I am personally concerned, he appears a little more often in these later years; he has remarkable vigor, a power of concentration and an amusing way of changing conversation.

I asked him the difference between East and West, where belief is concerned.

"The East," he tells me, "allows man to think for himself. The true Oriental perceives consciousness as something absolute behind which man may not go. The West purports to have a feeling that man can make prophets and alleged deities that support what is called spiritual knowledge itself. The wise ones see supreme consciousness as the key to all that exists. Their methods of teaching are entirely authoritative and traditional. The help of a guru from the East teaches that life is as a schoolroom through which man must pass and gives man the sense of being a part of nature's universal law."

I asked, "Are you then a part of that universal state of being?"

"Well," he answered, "man designs me in his own image. I am his servant and the carrier of his burden when he speaks of sin."

"What is sin?" I eagerly asked.

"Sin is anything that transgresses the code of theological honor held by man. There are therefore many aspects to its meaning, as man has made his own laws."

"Did Adam sin?" I asked him.

"I never knew man by that name, but all the universe moves eternally and so man thinks according to his devotion to knowledge."

There was silence as though my friend was impatient. It is a common and perhaps an instinctive practice to turn towards the indomitable will of nature: the thunder, the wind, the aspects of the Mother in all her caprice and change. Motiveless, Lucifer appears to know of the world but it troubles Him very little, and yet I realize men conceive of him as evil. Mentally he is alert and makes no demands on one's ability to believe in him.

In So Many Images

"Since you know me so well, you must know how often I want to speak to you of man's religious doubts and fear of dying. What have you got to say to me about it? You probably know that my attitude toward my own work is one that troubles many. On the one hand I have always 'seen' ghosts. As a child I was severely reprimanded for my spontaneous belief that there was no death, in the meaning with which the mourner believes; and as for you, I was always alleged to be close to you. My childish pranks, in hindsight, are suggestive of the fact that I am indeed closer to you than to God."

There was a long silence, followed by his answer delivered with serious intent: "Will you define for me what you mean? Are you in the mood to discuss belief? For Religion, as you use the word, will take a lifetime of discussion. In a few words I will set your mind moving in several directions.

"It is regretfully a fact that man has created me in so many images that I have long ago lost sight of my own identity. My opposite brother has less difficulty than myself; he remains where man has placed him, free from all material matters, filled with power over all—including myself—garmented in all that is good: perfect knowledge, faith, power and bliss, to be worshipped and remain forever divinely creative and created.

But I am as powerful, according to man, as the electrons and protons—his playthings for this contemporary moment in time.

"Terminology also divides us and keeps me busier than most people. To be the originator of sin sets up a terrific confusion, much easier than Reverence, sacredness, and holiness. These are kept in their respective boxes and rarely used."

I realized that I had touched on the psychological essence of life and that this mysterious virtue or force was telling me, half humorously, that the questions I wanted answered must be outside of symbolism and beyond the power of my friend to make me comprehend.

"You ask for Manna, my child," he said. "But that is not within the common process of a fool's paradise."

Nevertheless, the unanswered gave me a sense of relief. I was strangely happy to find myself once again alone.

A Sometime Optimistic Philosopher

I have been asked by my family how I converse with my "Noble Stranger." I very easily enter into a withdrawn mood. This happens to me often while other people are around, talking and generally having a good time. It appears that I slip away quite easily. To me it is a "detour" into nowhere. It has always been so. In my school days I got my knuckles rapped for being "willfully non-attentive." Nevertheless, these moments of "isolation" were not lost at another level. I perhaps heard music, a voice thinly quoting words of a well-beloved song. Always the stolen seconds are happy. It is possible that the "before and afterwards" take leave of the positive me.

It can happen in the midst of conversation: I can listen and at the same time pick up an unrelated subject for a brief interval. My mind continually works on two levels. Someone may be trying to lead up to a certain subject that he would have me believe. I listen, but that "otherness" follows the deeper meaning, while the other individual may congratulate himself believing I have been convinced and easily manipulated. As I have already had a quick glance at the whole picture, and since giving is the positive part of my relation to life, I have no personal struggle with myself. Conflicts, like bullets, fly around me at random, and thoughts are things to be accepted or rejected. Such a mind has often to pay a high price for its candor; my good friends very easily become enemies. I have had to suffer the faults of my own generosity but I cannot be less than myself.

Those like myself who see and yet must live the open, outgiving, ever-demanding service life, will understand the wounds that have to be borne by the too observant heart. For those, the few who must live without fear, know too well the high price that one pays for the gifts of knowing and seeing into and beyond. For such mentality, everything looks simple. One lives too close to the realities of the physical life to escape it, nor would one even if one could. Sunk in the stupidity of human love, one walks unthinkingly, guarded within by force of silence.

For these reasons I regard the "Noble Stranger" as one who may be the image of a cultured individual who has the moral advantage of a sometime optimistic philosopher.

There Are No Victors

He appeared in my room at daybreak on Friday, July 18, 1969. Habitually with early morning light I go downstairs, and soaking in the tranquility of the Provencal countryside I take my usual cup of tea.

This date I was arrested by his presence, puzzled, but I saw him very clearly. I welcomed him and said: "It is a long time since I have had a visit from you."

He replied: "Now, I am well aware of your conflicts of your desire to 'disappear' because of your constant pain."

I somewhat petulantly asked him: "Why then can't you do something about my intense arthritic pain?" and he told me:

88

"You had a man of your race, George Bernard Shaw, who explained that youth was wasted on the young. I would ask you to remember for yourself the numerous tumbles that you had during your experimental youth with motorcycles, and also how many times you hurt yourself badly by jumping and trying to outdo the young males in your class. I remember you were valiant and would say: 'Oh, this is nothing.' But when we become aged, the bills for our delinquencies have to be met. Besides I have heard you say that suffering is good for the soul. Therefore, why not remember this?"

There was nothing I could think to say.

He then cynically smiled and said: "Are you, like all the rest, aware of the foolishness that is going to take place in a few days? Three young well-trained men, who have almost forgotten their manhood so hard has been the training, will go to the moon."

I asked him: "What then?"

"Oh," he replied nonchalantly, "the usual folly. Everyone will run to get a flag, then women and children will turn out waving the colors." He told me, still cynically, that the President was going for an extended tour, ending in that squalid center of the world that most Americans would like to forget.

I knew without asking that he referred to Vietnam. I told him: "It would take me many hours of serious discussion to give you my point of view about Vietnam. I feel it was a great mistake and I suspect we have not the honesty of purpose to admit it."

In response he replied: "The Hamlet of that moment needed a new stage to cover up his iniquities regarding the young and very sick President. It is a wonderful thing to send men to a distant country to kill off other hard-working people, who, themselves, have still no idea why they are being extinguished."

I quickly reminded him that this must indeed be part of his work, and he told me very quietly: "No, I am here to stimulate men who live on this planet. I give them power, and they do the rest. There are two sides to every coin, otherwise the world would not continue."

I listened quietly and knew that I could have spoken words of great depth if I were not shaking inside. I told him: "Come and have a cup of tea with me; let's talk some more."

He said, "No, you have other work to do, and work is the solace of the universe."

Remaining rather British minded, I asked him if he would not go and wake up the British to remember that they once held great power.

He retorted: "They did have and used it too complacently. For a thousand years, or since they have been divided from the Continent, shall we say, they have armed to fight their neighbors and real relatives; for once they were a part of Europe. Because they were strong they have been accused of many iniquities and they have been mildly just. But now they feel that by being kind to all people they make a place for themselves. They are, in a sense, over-civilized, or so they think; so was Rome in her day, and when one lives only on memories, on what has been, life scuttles by—and they do not know the new values."

"Yet," I told him, "I am still very fond of Britain. At least tell me something good."

He answered: "They will survive."

I asked him again what he thought of the upcoming lunar episode and he said, "It is a courageous journey. I think the men who will make it will, for a few moments in time, feel themselves as kings; but after they have gone through the preliminaries of being made safe, they will be impossible to live with."

I said: "But have you no other word on this topic? What will it lead to?"

"Inevitably, war. Russia will not easily forgive, since she planted her flag there a decade ago," he said, "and the country is trained to believe that they will be eventually the victors."

Perplexed I tried to depart but he continued: "Of course, you know there are no victors. Man feeds himself with the image of power, and in that moment, he destroys himself."

"Have you no good word for the future?" I asked with trepidation.

"Not as long as you have foolish men ruling your governments."

I asked him: "But, do you not think that Monsieur Pompidou is good for France?"

He answered rather severely, "He will rock the cradle and preserve the equities; but France needs more and must have more since Germany hopes in her heart to win a battle against Russia, and when this starts, as it will, the whole of Europe will be involved."

Rather shocked I asked: "But, are you pleased about this?"

And he told me very quietly as he faded out: "No, my interest is to make man see his own weakness and profit thereby."

"Are you having any luck?" I queried.

"Not much. History repeats itself. But one day, after the blood has been shed, the flowers will grow again. Man will be a little holier for a moment, and then a new generation will say: 'Never again,' and a second generation will say: 'We are vigorous and strong: let us contain our enemies.'"

Our conversation at an end, I was ill for the rest of the day. I consider anew if he is an aspect of my own mind, or do I require and hence desire the image of his superior being with whom I can communicate? I continue to ponder and ask myself continually where lies the answer.

This Victorious Mirage

My "Noble Stranger" appeared again two days later, on the very morning when the three courageous astronauts undertook their visit to the moon. I asked him if they were in any danger.

"Yes and no. Accidents do happen, but these men have been so trained that it's essential that they make good. The philosophy that possesses them is not related to failure. The battles within are the most difficult: theirs is not to reason but to achieve. A spurious romanticism has taken over from instinctive intelligence. The enemy within has been conquered, as does the training for war. One must conclude that these gentlemen are the bearers of the banner of war. Those who will drool over the mission accomplished lightly think we have outsmarted the enemy. One must admit to oneself such monies were not thrown away for love and optimism. It is a tragedy of this moment in time that the economic riches of the contestants have carried man's distrust to the limit. The disaster then can come from this Christian optimism, and this victorious mirage can be the forerunner of the devastation of man. The end product in the foreseeable future leaves one pessimistic as to human destiny, be he Christian or Marxist. Christianity is aged and drifting away on a new river, and the sacrifice of Socrates will be a doctrine without significance."

Through the moon flight weekend of worshipping these heroes, I felt deeply unhappy. They are not free, these three fighters. One thinks of their inner shrinking from the brutality of the festive greetings that will be thoughtlessly offered them from the favored cities as a welcome home. Tired, numbed after three weeks of captivity, a few days of outer delight and inner tension, as they "bravely" set out to receive welcomes and decorations, filled with hysteria and discomfort while their bodies resist and their minds rebel. For the world, it is a spectacle; but for them surely an inner rebellion, and victory becomes in the end something more akin to revenge. If we could have the money lavished on the waste and spoilage of their good spirits into a fund that would enable them to relive their days before their obsessive training—and monies to assure their children's future—a grateful image would emerge and the welcome would be less than combat.

I asked him why he had come to me. "Are you delighted, surprised, or not particularly interested in the moon flight? The boys who make the journey surely demand admiration."

"There are several motives involved here," he replied. "I note your President will make himself noticeable. His henchmen will make it clear to him that his presence as one of the people would add luster to his faded image. Running away to Vietnam is a foolish effort since America cannot admit that her entry into Asia was a foolish and worthless effort. It is easy to sacrifice the lives of thousands of men if you are certain to achieve History and, of course, you will ultimately be responsible and held to account. But he missed his chance. When the records are written that Nixon did not admit 'It was foolish to step into Asia, I will take the troops home,' the pages that will one day note his Presidency will not provide him an exalted place in history."

I questioned: "I gather you do not think well of the President Nixon?"

"No, I do not. Like a meal presented that has been presented a long time ago, it lacks vital nourishment."

"Is he not somewhat more reasonable to the crowd than our late President Kennedy?"

"Not as outwardly greedy and vicious, but he has a false humility while the other one was, like most women with whom he was closely akin, never quite managing to cover his obscenities."

I changed the subject. "Will the courageous men who hope to reach the moon return?"

"Yes," he answered, "they will suffer the hellish welcome of being bored to death, pelted with choking dirt thrown by hysterical people, hurried to other places to be given inferior food, and tired out by what is known as welcome; but privately they do not enjoy this form of madness. Trust funds set up for their families and those who will follow, this would be the correct way to give thanks for their military victory, and no demands that they be seen when they really should relax. Forget that slice of earth that has given poets inspiration and lovers a mystique—an illusion that fades in this technological foolishness. That slice of eroded soil is now borne down again with man's foolish efforts: she has become infested with man's garbage. In the all-seeing universe, man continues to kill his brother for a religion that has far too many complicated objectives, and that makes no sense to an intelligent and colossal universal whole, beyond man's comprehension."

His words were more than prophetic, for days later it was hinted than an alliance could take place between Russia and America to stop the menace that is China.

The Fever of Non-Being

Two mornings later I heard my door open, but I thought it was the wind, as a strong gale from the North was blowing. I closed the door and there, inspecting my desk, was the "Noble Stranger."

I asked him quite sharply: "Will rampant forest fires destroy le Midi? Is it to your interest to see this beautiful land destroyed by so many fires? Even the American journalists are appalled that all these ancient villages, which combine to make up the French Riviera, are threatened with disaster. These villages represent for me the fine structural planning of our ancestors!"

Unfeelingly he replied: "These ancient villages placed on the hills were equivalent to the tanks of the last war carnage. One saw the movements of the other clans' chiefs—or neighbors, as you prefer to designate them. The wiser the headman, the greater his superiority in the eyes of his people."

I asked him: "Do you conceive of a day when man, devoid of fear, will live harmoniously with his neighbor?"

He replied: "Your charity is your great weakness, your generosity destroys you, your 'heroism' enables you to be instinctively able to hide the pain which keeps you imprisoned in body. The intoxication of your faith permits that you regard man's world as beautiful. Your private and secret hope, undeclared, would be to write the romantic life of the country, which unfortunately exists in fragments too minute to discover.

"If there is any good in the Universe, tranquility reigns, but not for long. Man has his dual nature: he has the components with which to live, as has nature. Temperament changes. The force and laws of nature have to be observed. The temperament for the make-up of each human is dual. It is therefore for each being to find himself and, so doing, he grows from infancy to old age. To navigate the frail corps of body takes each and all through experience. Temperament guides one through the waters of experience. The ritual of life is difficult for each. Each one has a duty to perform. Yes," he added, "that is the purpose behind life."

"Do we have a choice before we are born as to whether we shall remain in the pool of becoming, or is the choice ours?"

"The fever of non-being must be charged continually with the desire for oneness with the unknown. He who is unready may return to take another chance, one that may steer him through the currents of life to experience being the self. The unborn arrives at his moment of insistence for selfhood."

"May it not be possible," I enquired, "for one to go through life fearful of thus adding little to the picture of becoming one's self?"

"That," he replied, "requires many answers and many lives, since the goal is to find perfection and then, returning that state of perfection which is all knowing. One must reach a state of all knowing before he reaches the water of perfection."

"Do you believe in capital punishment?" I enquired.

"No man can say he has the right to pronounce death for another; however, man may have broken the laws of his brothers. But it is not within the law that the tortures of such punishment is in the legal hands of an administration, to condemn man to be killed so that the law be served."

As I considered his statement I reached for clarification. "How does man justify law as in the case of the late President of the United States? He is the respecter of the law."

He laughed, which rarely happens. "There comes that time in a man's life when he assures himself that he is the dispenser of justice. He does not think that all such lawless acts bring their repercussions. It is easy for a man who has risen to such heights to believe in his own glory and to be able to commend death for a nation; he is in the judgment seat in his own blindness and cannot conceive of being at fault."

"Is there in the evolutionary scheme no judgment?"

"Yes, the moment man breaks the law to dispense justice, his inner self must from then, through infinite time, suffer and continue to make mistakes. It is better for such a one that he had not been born, for while he accumulates riches, they are as ashes. Outwardly he must maintain a look of enjoyment before his fellow men, but the price must be paid and death does not make him less a terrified animal."

My Kingdom is Part of Growth

As autumn made its presence in the South of France, feeling ill I had a curious revelation: the lady who gives of her time to help me keep my correspondence and writings in order advised me that, in her estimation, it was I who called the Nobel Stranger to me, as I continually bombarded him with questions. I realized that perhaps I might be the guilty one, complicit in keeping our contact. Hence, I decided to cease to rely on him.

Reading the Sunday papers and contemplating the ongoing troubles that plague my homeland of Ireland, I reflected back to my childhood when I was a curious and demanding girl. I recalled conversations with George William Russell[26], fondly known as A.E. If there was indeed a continuum of life after death, I reflected upon how he would, from the celestial sphere he inhabits, regard Ireland's most recent and continuing tragic infighting between Catholic and Protestant. It was from his lips that I learned of Madame Blavatsky. "Beware," he once told me, "as you grow up never to cross her path. She was a curious woman. Your eyes give me an impression of being in some stage of life related to her." (This is a comment I have heard often in

---

[26] George William Russell (1867-1935) was a writer, poet, Irish nationalist, mystic. He moved in literary circles with James Joyce and William Butler Yeats, and was one of the original members of the Theosophical Society.

relation to a similar resemblance of our eyes). He would proudly proclaim that he was a theosophist, though a poor one at that, but that Madame Blavatsky was a formidable presence and that I should keep clear of her doctrine.

I was to recall his words, then unintelligible to me, when I met Annie Besant[27] herself though G.R.S. Mead, in the days when my mediumistic work caused me to work with him. Mead was a gracious individual who had known and worked with Blavatsky and felt that my mediumship opened a door to her spiritual presence. This continued for eleven years until I had a sad letter from him, written from Sark, a little island that had become his summer retreat. He loved my daughter very dearly and talked with her as he took her to the cinema regularly. He often spoke to me of Satan whom he regarded as a good fellow who could quote the Scriptures, who was given a bad name by the women who have no idea of peace in the heart, and tempt away from the divine law. Laughter within and peace bring stillness. Even now I felt his grandeur of spirit: a bearded saint with eyes that laughed behind glasses that never hid youth and humor.

With my mind lost in a youthful past, I returned from my reverie to find my austere friend Lucifer beside me.

"This is a day of rest," he told me. "Did not your able teachers of your youthful days command that work be set aside and Sunday be given over to the praise of the Holy Family?"

"Does it concern you?" I replied.

"Yes, and no. You must remember that man has inhabited the planet for a million years, during which time he has had many idolic images."

"Have you been there all that time?"

"Yes, of course. Man has been too fearful to talk directly to the Divine Presence; but, as Moses needed his weak brother

---

[27] Annie Besant (1847-1933) was a social activist championing women's rights, education, and independence for Ireland and India. She was a President of the Theosophical Society, and author of numerous works on Hinduism, mysticism, the afterlife, and the occult.

to gratify man's weakness, I was their creation. But remember well, on the long journey to perfection my kingdom is part of growth."

"Why, when you have the world almost continually on the brink of war, do you trouble to come to converse?"

"You are talking to your external being and have clothed me as to your heart's desire."

"Are you telling me you are a figment of my inner need to converse with someone who can keep my mind occupied?"

"There are many answers to your question," he admitted, "but why did you not devote your life to writing?"

"That is a good question and I can answer you easily. My early experience at school gave me the opportunity to meet great poets and great writers. With the exception of James Joyce whom I did not like, and Yeats who visited me in London once, I revered the unique group of writers, poets, and thinkers as a special group of superior beings. I have not done anything that would give me the right in my own mind to intrude on a world that knew intimately women of the caliber of Maud Gonne[28], Lady Gregory[29] and the shrewd but quiet lady who was the wife of George Russell[30]. In those far-off days, the young were wise enough to know greatness and quality of mind, and observe silence and respect. Yeats was a believer in spiritualism and I was only partially caught in the web when I knew him, which later on engulfed my whole life."

---

[28] Maud Gonne (1866-1953) was an Anglo-Irish actress involved in the suffragette movement and Ireland's fight for independence. She was also W.B. Yeats's long-time paramour and muse.

[29] Lady Gregory (1852-1932) was an Irish playwright who founded two theaters with W.B. Yeats, and an author of retellings of Irish folktales and mythology.

[30] Violet North (1869-1932) was a theosophist and part of the Irish literary revival, who, like Lady Gregory, wrote works inspired by Irish legends under the pseudonym "Laon." Her sole book, as Violet Russell, was *Heroes of the Dawn: Stories of Fionn and the Fianna* (Maunsel & Roberts, Dublin: 1922).

As I busily formulated my continued response I suddenly realized he had taken his leave.

The Broader Vision

I wanted to walk in the Autumn sunshine but something held me in my office. It had long been on my mind to seriously ask the "Noble Stranger" about the years I spent in the world of ghosts and hauntings. I realized that in the Autumn of my life, my questions remained unanswered. My preoccupation with the subject of so-called psychic functioning apparent in my life and in that of others has been, in times of reflection, the eternal puzzle to which I seek solution and true meaning. I have dedicated my lifetime to finding answers to the questions raised by psychic phenomena.

I have always been in the curious position of being detached from the subject and yet very solicitous that I treat it factually. My early training was long, and did not permit me to dwell on the negative aspects of the work that held me, even when I knew that I was waging a blind battle with myself.

Once I had decided to enter seriously into something that I knew nothing about, the battle was drawn and commenced. My cautious self was always in evidence, but the inner or subjective mind had its own point of view and spontaneously took over. My objective detachment served me well. I had the sense to know that the spontaneous me would keep to its own territory—and it has continued to do so, even though at the end of my life I remain so heavily committed to my work for increased understanding of the universe.

The arthritis that I continually suffer saps my onetime magical flow of energy which is regretful, but my other perceptive side serves me well and enables me to accept graciously my fate most of the time. Even when my pain is out of control, the inner being takes over to defeat what could at times defeat me.

The broader vision prevails and beckons.

To Join the Living Breath of the Planet

I asked my remaining questions of my esteemed companion. "What do you think of my life's work? What do you have in mind regarding the question of survival after death? Solidarity against death?"

"Your religious trainings," he replied, "Must have given you answers. They have believed in the death penalty, sincerely hoping—I will not say believing—that there is another world where one has another chance to seek forgiveness."

"Do you believe it?" I asked very pointedly.

"Frankly, no." he replied. "Life goes out at death to join the living breath of the planet. There is neither below nor beyond. Man has evolved to have mind, which obviously confuses him! He believes he has power over all the earth, while the rest of evolution gives each other form of life an instinct that protects all over life, to keep alive and teach far beyond man in sensitivity and care for their young. Man interferes with his own growth when he acts as though he has the powers of life and death in his own hands. So long as he deceives himself, he cannot evolve patiently and may one day regress.

"One day. In the not too far future, man will destroy life for himself and other animals."

In desperation I implored "But where are all the sacred promises gone that once gave the illusion of peace? Where is the mystery of life and the magic of love? Why do you envision such a bitter ending?"

"It is obvious that man has the ability to destroy. One day the accident will happen. He has turned the vital sources of life into weapons of destruction—enough to obliterate his kind. No one knows the hour, but I must come because there is fear and resentment in the heart of mankind."

BOOK TWO

LUCIFER'S COMPENDIUM OF GUIDANCE

On First Working with Universal Law

You know there is this to be said: that the moment you put your feet into universal law, you are bound to have many, what you will call, conflicts all within yourself; and not to be disheartened if at first there are these protests against the method of your working or dealing with things, but rather to acquiesce in the disappointments and yet make up your mind that the disappointments can be changed to the niceties, if only you will hold firm.

Fundamental Principles

There is only one underlying principle in life, and that is that you cannot pay duty to the God-consciousness of the Universe in whatever form that appeals to you unless you first pay duty to yourself. After all, you are a spark of this little, magnificent God-consciousness. Not by accident are you here today. This time is right and wise for you, as right and wise as the day of your entrée into this Universe. Everything that you do is a negation or an affirmation of God, equally much as an affirmation of yourself. You are a spark of the first principle. Believe me, you have come to this stage of knowing and being because you have understood the evolutionary lesson and you have by your own understanding conquered each obstacle or you would not be here. It is the first moment in the history of your soul that you become, as it were, the God of the Universe, capable of pronouncing life and death, capable of giving life of yourself, capable of giving death of yourself.

In this great moment, therefore, it seems a tragedy that man, the noblest of God's consciousness that you know, should so often beset himself with ridicule and responsibilities. He will do things today that he would not have done at any period of his evolution. Always it has been struggle without strife that the self may dominate. And this life should be struggle with the life that the self, which is the soul, should dominate but dominate in security, not dominate in aggression. And the principle behind every word that I have ever spoken to you has been that you can only glorify the God-consciousness—you can only glorify the highest ideal within you—I care not whether you are Mohammedan, Buddhist, Christian or pagan—you can only glorify that ideal by understanding duty—not to anyone in the Universe but duty to yourself; for if you know duty to yourself, my friend, not in words but in deep meaning, you do nothing but render to each man that which is his due. You do not render it in responsibility. You render it in giving.

You are always seeking, as is all mankind, for an explanation of God. He has drawn it in every essence of the Universe. He has given you eyes and ears that you may see and hear. He has given you the expression of touch that you may say it is not an illusion of the senses. Behold, it is true! He has given you an affinity with all things. He has given to you the eternal sun and the moon and the stars and the beneficence of their love for the earth. If the earth ever once did other than accept the graciousness of this beneficence, she would fall into chaos. If she ever said "No" but wisely accepted and wisely gave, there would be chaos in the Universe. If in the duty of the water and the air and the elements and the life of the elements there is rebellion, such rebellion is immediately stamped out by rightness in thinking. You do not find in the beehive that there is rebellion. Each one does his share—even gives of life unto glorious death with beautiful acceptance. You do not find anywhere in the whole world the mistakes that man has never made till this moment when he is looking for a God-consciousness that exists within himself, and exists plentifully and beautifully in everything around him. Believe me, my child, there is no word that I speak with you that does not contain the fundamental philosophy of knowing God's Universe.

On Acquiring Passivity

The first important step towards passivity is to rest some few minutes of the 24 hours each day—the longer the better. In a busy life, it is difficult to set moments aside. I am never tired of emphasizing this, first, last and always. One cannot begin to criticize the intelligence of our neighbors until we understand ourselves. These few moments I call washing and cleansing of the mind—so that the soul may operate more freely through the body, the body which is the temple of the soul. This may seem a waste of time, but only through peace is this attained and can one know the God essence.

Allow the mind to cease to work. Still the body. Allow the nerve activity of the body to relax. Breathe so that the body gains oxygen for enrichment. Take rest—completely. Begin to empty the mind. Do not seek peace through meditation or concentration. Both bring the conscious mind into play. The rightful attitude to rest is either out flat or in a sitting position like the Buddha, or with the spinal column relaxed. Permit all vestige of thought to go from you. When you are not thinking, all vestiges, all inconsistencies pass away. You will see the inner mind like a crystal bowl. In two weeks, you will get results if you do this regularly.

Before relaxation make a demand on the universe. I advisedly do not use the word prayer. To the western mind, prayer is a formula. Your last conscious thought should be "I do this that I may understand the universe in which I live, that I may understand myself, that I may take to myself with conscious knowing this healing and understanding of God. It is necessary that I should know the God of me. I beg that I may live myself to the essence of God and so understand it in myself, and in the universe." You cannot find the reality and help without permitting the mind complete passivity. When you begin to see little patterns and winding roads within yourself you will ask for knowledge to interpret these things.

In your daily life, my friend, do it with exhilaration. Do not hide your face from the universe. The bowing of the head is what is called reverence. Do not do this. Throw back your head—let your inner eye pray to the universe. When you pray—ask—everything you do in the day—do it as though it meant something of stimulation in your life. Only by such method do you bring usefulness into your method of work.

Q: *Each night, before going to sleep, I have tried to carry out your suggestion in order to obtain passivity but I have difficulty.*

I say to you, the failure there, my friend, is in the emphasis on your own statement, "I have tried." Passivity is a state of mind, which comes literally with the ability to be able to relax the nervous system. I do not like to use the word "try." Forgive me for saying this, because if you try to make yourself passive, it means you are still using the conscious patter. If we attempt, or as you put it yourself, *try* to achieve a state of concentration, we are concentrating. The faculty or the method is not concentrating. It is akin to letting down all of the muscular activities almost as though you were going to settle for sleep. It is a relaxation of your thoughts. As long as the conscious mind plays any part, it is useless. Many people will tell you that concentration is essential to passivity. As long as you concentrate, think, or make effort at all, there is no passivity. Passivity amounts to an ability, therefore, to be able to relax and think not at all.

Q: *I try completely physically, emotionally, nervously to relax in every way for a short period, making my mind apparently blank, but thoughts begin to creep in and I have extreme difficulty in keeping outside thoughts from coming in.*

Are then the outside thoughts useful?

Q: *They are just the thoughts of the day. They are impertinent shall we say.*

The first law of self-help or self-development is the ability not to think with the conscious mind. Do not relax without motive before the utter relaxation sets in. Permit that the soul escapes—permit that the consciousness is going to be perfectly at peace and that the attempt is made for a very definite reason: that the soul, instead of giving its thoughts to the body and to the activities of the day, shall speed itself into the greater universe of thought, of philosophy, and of the kind of helpfulness that you most desire. Of course, for a little while you are bound to have some thoughts flowing across, but bit by bit, bit by bit they will, as the mind sinks to restfulness, cease to become troublesome. It is a difficult thing to get the conscious mind to change its activity, so that you may have a protest in it over this; but it is worthwhile to get over the protest, and I am perfectly certain that what you will gain in inner receptivity from such refreshment will truly be worth the effort.

Q: *Should I then have faith in what I find if that passivity may be brought about?*

That is the most difficult stage, because in this, your western orientation, time and its consequence seem of such utter importance to you—even when, it seems to me, you get the time I do not know that you always use it to the best of your ability. I can talk more glibly of this because the passage of time does not have the same consequence for me, and therefore I do not live in the same essence as you do. Realizing that time is endless, it is not, therefore, essential that I irritate myself with it as you do. I do believe, however, that the essential difference between the west and the east is that this timelessness is not taught to the child at all. You will notice that the very young child, before being spoilt by the conventional attitude, has no theory of time at all, and can lapse easily away from you and live on the verge of this outer universe. But it is the "Listen to me!" to the continual command behind it, that spoils forever the ideal of rest, and that is what is essential to you. The more active you are, my friend, the more energy you burn. It is therefore in your case more essential that utter relaxation should be arrived at—not only for the soul stimulus. Not only is it imperative that each human being should have this moment, as he has in sleep, but it is a chemical necessity to the whole of your body. I advocate it in the most practical way for you.

Further Questions Concerning the Process of Becoming Passive

Q: *In seeking passivity, fleeting thoughts keep coming into my consciousness. I am also conscious of my breathing and occasionally my heartbeat.*

Well, that is good. At least you know that you breathe and you know that you have a heart. It is good that you should listen for the sounds of your own body. It is good that you should recognize the body as a machine by the fact that you hear the breathing. Bit by bit you will begin to hear the activities of the body. How can you listen to God's Universe and God's speech unless you first know the radiation of yourself? That is all part of the plan. But to *seek* passivity, this is incorrect. Passivity comes upon you through these activities. You do not seek it. The very fact you can forget the outside world to hear your breathing, to hear your heart—it is pounding like that all the time. You are breathing like that all the time. But you are so busy with the externals that you do not realize or know it. While seeking passivity while hearing these things, you are listening to yourself for the first time in your life.

Q: *Is it then all right for me to be conscious of the fact that I am listening to myself?*

Is it not a beautiful thing to think that you can listen to your machinery? To the mechanism of yourself, for bit by bit that finer, deeper understanding will come when you will know that the mechanics speak and act through you. Then you will know that the mechanics of the God-consciousness are also then speaking to you.

Q: *In contemplation, I have at times seen pictures of a sunset with a series of lines like the bright edges of clouds. I have also seen at times what looked like bright sky through silvered hued woods. When I experience similar impressions should I let my mind think about them?*

Do not think of them. Let them pass in perspective. It shows that the inner understanding is attuning itself with the method of visioning. If you see the sky, remember that the inner eye has not seen the sky in that perspective, but it knows that it must if it is to be useful to you, so it shows that it is attuning its vision to your objective vision that you may see in perspective as rightly as you see with a lens. If you see the perspective of sky through wood with the inner eye, remember that the inner eye is using the objective vision so that it may attune itself to this. What you see with the inner eye is not seen in form. It is seen rather in rhythm and formlessness. The fact that you are seeing these things is very good. It shows that your consciousness is responding and that you are having an alignment of this in the very things that appear to you.

Q: *I experience, as if my eyes are trying to focus, a strange effect in my eyes—my left eye is not focusing quite as my right eye. It is if I struggle slightly, going on even when I think my whole mind is free of the thoughts of the world and thoughts of the day.*

Well, there may be just a little elemental something in your objective vision and your spiritual vision is trying to align itself to it. Be watchful of these things because you then presume to see things in your objective body that you have never been aware of, and you will then see the struggle with the spiritual eye is not a struggle indeed but an idea to attune itself to the difficulties that it finds in the body physical. This is all right. This draws your attention to the figments of yourself with which you have been quite familiar and that did not seem to be in any sense wrong to you. Yet the fact that the spiritual vision has to be attuned to them shows that there is something there to be attending itself.

Q: *Do I assume that I shall just continue with my quiet periods every day?*

Absolutely. This is essential for you. They are not only essential to you for your own peace of mind, but he is a wise general, who, after all, has taken thought of the road he sends his troops. He may not see all the obstacles by visioning the road day by day because he cannot see the obstacles that a hidden enemy may produce, but at least he knows the obstacles on the road which makes him able to deal with the outside attack, and you cannot ever deal with tomorrow by rushing into it today. One must see the day in perspective, and not think it into being, but see it, and seeing get some line of action on the road. You can only do this, therefore, by having the mind completely washed out and attuning it to direction. So it is not only that it is good for your spiritual values—it is essentially right and wise for the physical you. You should really train the mind every day to have rest. You throw your body down and let it relax and then turn the mind loose into all kinds of obscure pathways. You should not do that. It is essential to let the mind rest. It adds to longevity, it adds to peace, it adds to wisdom, and it adds to the rightness of your decision process.

Technique of Getting Help from the Universe

Q: *If I understand correctly, what is mine from the universe I always have within my reach—help and advice from the universe to answer any question which may arise?*

Yes, any question. Any question that may arise is a human problem. Therefore, it is the problem of the universe. There is no question that can arise that cannot be looked at with perfect serenity and answered with perfect magnificence.

The most important step is to perfect the complete relaxation of man's tense conscious nature and to eliminate bondage such as indigestion—lack of exercise—anything that tends to upset your whole equilibrium.

Five moments per day spent in the most delightful way of stretching the body will help you. The particular one, which gives to the body such graceful effect, is the drawing in of oxygen, and then going down and utterly relaxing. The attitude for that is to draw in good draughts of fresh air and then let the body go, so that you press out of the abdomen all the nitrogen and hydrogen and carbonic acid gas that stays in the fissures and pockets of the lower lung, which is the diaphragm. That diaphragm, if it is the least inflated, presses against the heart and that in turn also interferes with the sac, the stomach. Therefore, to me this is the most ideal, and if you will think of the Oriental at prayer you will notice that he has the tendency to bend himself to the ground. Now that eliminates all the carbons that will otherwise cling to the body, and if you do this three or four times, you understand that it pulls the muscles of the spinal column into effect. It releases all the adhesive quantity in the kidney. It gives to it greater energy. It presses the liver. It must if utter relaxation sets in, and it is like the action of a sponge. If there is absorption, it also causes pressure, not much but a little, which will infuse this out or take it out of the system. It is the simplest of all exercises and it is the best I can offer you in occult law, but when you draw up again you draw in your oxygen and by the force of that oxygen pump out the hydrogen, nitrogen, and carbonic acid gas.

It is essential for the human being to stretch himself. It is that way that you keep the muscles taut, and the time will come, my friend, if you think as I think you are going to, when you will need to express yourself in that way—when no day will pass that you do not give joy to the body. You see, it works both ways. You could not let a day pass without a little play; that is essential to loosen the body. You waste so much effort during the day and yet you give no effort to the relaxation of your tired muscles. How many moments would this take from your day? Yet, what great health you will see given to you.

Demand and Responsibility

You must put your demand out to the Universe with all earnestness—it is your need and just as necessary for you as the cup of water that you drink to allay your thirst. If you have the right to take that from the faucet of life, you have the right to ask for help. Always you have the right. Rightly or wrongly, you have the right. I do not care what you ask for. The only account is this: that if you ask for death on your neighbor, consciously desiring his death, you do that taking full responsibility, because it may be like a boomerang and come back. I do not care what you do so long as you take the responsibility. You break the law, however, the law of kindliness, the law of self—you break that when you reach out consciously to hurt or to destroy. But if in the principle of reaching out, destruction comes and you had not meant that, that is all right. That law I cannot propound often enough to you.

Present Your Plan to the Universe

Q: *Certain friends owe me money, which if repaid to me now, would enable me to continue with the plans I have in mind.*

*Would you counsel that in the midst of my busy day, I should
quietly withdraw and let my conscious self leave me, let thinking
leave me, to try to reach the state of total passivity within which
the solution may occur to me?*

Yes, but before, my friend, there is the recognition that you want
this money from your several friends. Therefore, before you sit
to the passivity, directing the soul, direct work for yourself.
"Now, before I am going to relax utterly, relax into this state of
passivity, here is my plan," which you present to the universe.
"I want, for my development, that this friend should do this
and this friend shall do that." And you leave that out on the
universe and let the soul then escape to gather philosophy and
knowledge for its next important step. There is the demand to
the Universe, my friend. If that is God, and I am God, here is
the relationship. If I am to become as great as that Universe
and I am that becoming, then if the law that operates in that
it is operating for all that is right and good, of a necessity it
is operating for me. So you put yourself within the rhythm of
security. You do see my point?

You must not only have the passivity—you must always
have the demand. Otherwise, my friend, you are sitting down
in the midst of a desert. The conscious thinking is "This is my
demand. This is my force."

Relax and let the soul get out to receive the security that it
needs, so that it may deal with the next important life lesson.
But above all, you, the individual, are becoming confident so
the demand must be made. It is not enough that you say, "Well,
here I am, wandering around the face of the earth. Take my
problems." That is wrong and futile. That is the great tragedy
behind all idealistic thinking. I am not giving you an ideal. I
am giving you an individual security—and if you have that,
believe me you have many ideals.

Take the Universe Into Your Confidence

If you are going to talk to the Universe, you have got to take the Universe into your confidence. You might say, "I want the farm moved." The Universe will say, "Why?" "Well, because after all I have done the best I can with it. Frankly, I have not done much. I want to be rid of it because my interest in it has waned. I want to move in other directions. I want it to be moved." That is the way to speak to the Universe. And move it will. That is a demand and reasonable logic. If you are going to talk to a man—your father, your mother, who asks you for the answer to a certain thing—you will try to the best of your ability to give your reasons for moving. Well, give your reasons to the Universe, which hears all, sees all, and supplies all. The man who merely implores, saying "God help me!" is making a great mistake. Nobody has heard him. He has just made another useless request that has no meaning.

Starting the Day Right

Q: *Would it be advisable to have a complete relaxation in the beginning of every day in order to put my thinking for the day in harmony with the Universe?*

I can only answer you that by telling you of the Chinese philosopher who said that the night was given up to thinking anyway, but that the day was given up to activity. He arose with the dawn so that he might begin to find the impatience in man's beginning life and thereby profit.

Each man starts out almost with a protest to his day's work. You know that is true. He therefore sets about his day by turning the rhythm of life against him. If he could only for a moment lift his hands to the Universe and say, "The day, oh God, is good. I, myself, am well," and move in this fashion, forgetting the impatience of mankind—the day would be good. That is the answer.

Now you would not go out and meet your neighbor with a hand that carries with it the grime and toll of yesterday. You would not think it was seemly to go, shall we say, to your first engagement unless you would have performed your morning ablutions. If you did, you would apologize, I am certain. But it would not have been your frame of mind to do this. Nor would it have been your frame of mind to meet a man of importance in the soiled clothes of yesterday. Yet you apparently do go out with your mind all steamed up, with the thinking of yesterday. It is important to every human being, I care not who he is, to take a moment with himself for conscious clarification, and therein dedicate his conscious or unconscious desire to manifest to the best within himself throughout every day. It is important. The bell from the mosque does not ring in vain, my friend, and often you will make fun, in the west, of the man who takes to his praying carpet at the sound of the bell. There is a method behind it. Pause a while in the early morning and during the middle of the day and in the evening relaxing in the same fashion as in the name of the Prophet. Relax and again you ask—for prayer is but demand.

Eliminating Tension

The tension of contact makes for a difficulty in expressing that which is within one, and even a difficulty in hiding the thing that you do not wish to express. There is no tension in security, my friend, but there is unusual calm—the tension must, of a necessity, move out the moment security comes in. You are only, after all, intense about anything when you do not know about it, is it not so? If a man comes into your office in a tense frame of mind, is it not as though you were going to meet an enemy? Is the tension not a protest against the day's activities to begin with? The moment that you become keyed up and withdrawn, have you not protested against life? If you jump into the water in such a frame of mind, the water is not going to be good; but if you open yourself up full well knowing that here is a day of creation for you, there is no need for tension.

The very method of thinking by which we assume security is surely going to do away with the tensing of nerves and muscles which destroy from the very beginning any joy we may get out of the day's work. The best thing to do is to relax in the early morning and take a joy in your ability to get ready for the day's work. If it is a little exercise I do not mind. I do not care what it is that opens you up, but see and feel yourself.

Prepare yourself in such a way and when the day comes, what are you afraid of? It is nothing. You are going to swim in, confident in the thought "I am secure," and if you know you are going to enjoy it, my friend, you do not protest against it. The lack of tension comes with the understanding of the method of approach to the law of governing your work. The one releases the other. If there is no insecurity, what do you protest against? Hence there is no protest.

You Cannot Live Tomorrow Today

If you are going to let your soul operate for you and you have an appointment at ten o'clock tomorrow, nothing that you think at ten o'clock tonight is going to be of any advantage at ten o'clock tomorrow because ten o'clock tomorrow is not yet born. It is in the womb of time. The circumstances connected with it are not ready. So why do you bring tonight's thinking to tomorrow's birth? And anyway the concept that you model tonight will practically be of no use tomorrow. Tomorrow will bring its own answer, and it will only bring its answer if you take your hands off it and leave it alone. Oh, you are all so inclined to say "If only." Let the "If onlys" go. The fact is this: things are as they are because you did not know, because you did not have today's experiences to deal with yesterday. And today's experience cannot deal with tomorrow's question. But it *can* deal with today's. And if it has dealt with today's rightly, then you may take it for granted that it will deal with tomorrow's when tomorrow's comes.

You may have a point of view and may vacillate between solutions. But that is enough. You have a set appointment for three o'clock. It is enough that you have set the plan. It is enough that you have committed yourself to the meeting. But do not also come with yesterday's words, for yesterday's words are as dead as yesterday and with a million years ago already. Make your date and forget it. What are you going to say to that man that you meet? What do you know that is in his mind? What can you bring out today for tomorrow or a week hence when a thousand intervening thoughts and actions will change his and your point of view in the interim? Let the moment that you meet him decide. Build, if you like, the skeleton of the house, but please do not furnish it before the house is built. Make the appointment and when you get there bring your thinking capacity to bear. If you have written down your thoughts, when you arrive your mind will be confused with this and that and the other and you will not be able to communicate successfully. By making the appointment and then forgetting about it until your arrival you will save energy. It will also save your time and your peace of mind, and it is going to permit you to use the inspiration that God gives you, from moment to moment out of this divine Universe, to bring the inspiration of the moment to the moment's problem, not to bring something second-rate or third-rate that you have cooked up and served to him cold.

The Value of Non-Attention

Do not turn attention to the matter at hand and give it more value than it ever possessed. When you think about a thing in concentration, you make it valuable and you also cause other people to think about it. Therefore, when you want to win in a case like that, forget it. If you want the depreciation to be there, do not think of what it may become. You are giving it life. If you think constantly about it, surely somebody will catch your thought and that thought becomes then a duality of thought and somebody else will catch it and give to it a value that it does already possess. Relax on it; forget it. It is as though it does not live at the moment. In this manner you will in time succeed.

Diplomacy

Make no plans when you want to test your enemy's fire. Do not give him any idea that you are even going to do such a thing. Stroll in and ask questions. If the diplomats of the Universe, instead of writing notes to each other warning each one to beware, try. Because you know very well if you give them any warning of what is in your heart, or you write anything or you speak anything in any formal attitude, he is immediately on his guard. You can go and see him with the most cordial outlook in the world extended to him and his friends, and you can get him to speak his plans. But if you go with a note of "I am suspicious," he would take up that suspicion and you would find nothing. So go to eulogize, and if you ask questions he is off his guard. Now, that is the rule for all moments of diplomacy.

Q: *May I express during negotiations that I do not like the way things are progressing?*

You can during your negotiations express disappointment, but not that you do not like something as then you would give him a loophole. Keep the other fellow's idealism intact and tell him you have been disappointed a little. This mention of disappointment will bring out a "for instance." He will probably ask you what are your disappointments and then you will say "this and this, but maybe I expect too much, or my mind sees too far ahead." In any case, do not lay blame. Only speak of the idealism that has not come true. Let that be your attitude.

Beware of Confidential Communications

I do not advise the idea of writing confidential notes. There is no such thing in the world as a confidential note. The moment you think that you write something in confidence, and that the necessity is there, then you are playing into the league of an enemy. You may feel that this is a confidential note. He may regard it as a confidential note. You do not know what will crop out in two hours that will make that of less confidence! The moment that the necessity arises for such confidences between people who have any knowledge of this at all, then they are playing a losing hand.

The only way to deal with problematical questions is oral speech. State it and preferably alone. Then nobody can ever say, "You said this; but my dear friend, a year ago you wrote me this." Most of the murder and confusion in the Universe hangs on this confidential note. Remember that. Speech only. This is a principle for all life. The moment that you have at any time of your life said, "Now I am going to write to that fellow in confidence"—just change it and state, "I must get that man to talk with." And have nobody else present. The words must die as they are spoken. Then, and then only, has the confidence been kept.

Making Use of Other People

I do not care with what branch of industry you are dealing at the moment. Each and every man, whether he is in a small, large, or greater scale, is ready to be used, because no man knows where the next day's policy is taking him. There is no deliberate thinking in any community at the moment, because each man has his hand on his own security and is likely to take that security this or that way. Do realize this and when you go to make these contacts, it is not what they want, it is what you can get to yourself. Now this may sound a very selfish policy, my friend, but I have no time for the fellow who stands on the street corner offering you sound advice and offering you security and begging you to make use of what he possesses, when his assets are nil. But I have much attention to pay, and so have you, to the man that you will meet on the other side of the street, who has looked to it that he has something to offer and that his well-being is there in the eyes of the Universe. You may be suspicious of him but you will approach him with respect, whilst there will be the look of contempt in your eyes for the unselfish one. You will realize that the one who looks well to the Universe is the one who has the power to help you.

And that is true. The Infinite has put you here, first, last, and always, to give just stewardship. If you take the things of the Universe, whatever they may be, it is right and just that the use of the Universe is yours. It has been given to you in beauty with all its content. You have been given a mentality by which to use and enjoy it. Ill-use of it ill-behooves you any good. Too much of it brings disaster. But the right use of it—the fundamental concept of right-using to yourself first, that you may give with sanity to each one and give with discrimination—that is stewardship. That is right. Not for self-glorification, not for the power that it gives to you, but for the ability at the end of the day to say, "I have made many mistakes, but since I have recognized Thou, oh God, within mine own self, I have rendered to Thy Universe help, to Thyself Thy servant, endurance; and to the process of Thy becoming, which is the process of evolution, just and important thinking."

If you will not go ahead with your plan my friend, you will find that some other personality will come and set up exactly that principle and you will stand aside and say, "If only I had done that!" That is the answer. Each man takes of the best he has and offers it to life. But he offers it knowing that he is giving of his best. That is the Law.

Q: *So to use a slang expression, "the Sky is the limit" and I should go ahead and execute my plans?*

Exactly, providing that you keep your feet very firmly in the earth of the Universe. By using this contact of security with every man that you meet, you are laying the basis of a new foundation. You know the old method of thinking. You meet your friend on the highroad of life. He says, "You are a very ill man." You begin to wonder. A little later on you meet another friend and he says, "My friend, time has dealt badly with you. You are aged." And you have only got to meet one other personality who tells you that you are ill and infirm and, you *are* that, and you know it is true. But if for a moment the day is good, and the first friend says, "Ah, but you are so well, you are so strong, you are vigorous," and the second friend should say, "How well that time deals with you," and the third says, "God is in your heart," you are an exalted man.

This is the process of thought that has changed you from the heaven of well-being to the hell of non-understanding. Do you see this? Therefore, as you meet your first contact of the day with security, you place your first foundation stone—well and securely laid. Then you present to him confidence in you when you believe, "That is good now. That is all right. I have met a man this morning who knew what he spoke of." Now do you see how the rhythm of it begins to move? But if you argue here and there and say, "No, not this, but this perhaps..." ah, it is wrong from the very beginning. It is like the foundation stone of life in your first approach to security. You cover whatever you may feel, and you give and give instinctually, but you give security and it is that and it is only that—your first approach— that lays for you the finer or the lesser foundation.

On Soliciting Donations

You have the birth of something that you believe in, otherwise you would not be doing it. You have enough altruism in your soul or enough experience of life in your soul—not one life but many—to make you realize that the best good is done by the individual in the amount of good that he bestows on the Universe as he goes through it. Is it not so? Now, if you see that point and it becomes an ideal with you, it is well that that garden shall be sown. But now you say to me, "I have not enough seed of my own, but I know through certain efforts of my own I may procure more." Now you ask me if you have the right to ask it. What I will say to you is this: You come into the Universe even without clothes. If you needed them you would have been born with them. You come in without anything but the security that the time is coming that you can make use of everything. You come in to render stewardship to the best of our ability. Now, to make this stewardship possible, sometimes you have to heal and sometimes you have to hurt. So long as you do not hurt consciously, it is well. What your actions bring unconsciously is not your responsibility. You are the weapon of Destiny.

The reason you are all hoarded here together is that by your very activity, one on the other, you refine that flesh that the God-consciousness may appear. Therefore, if there is a well of water and there is a garden in which there is seed, you are not going to steal it. You are going to walk up to your neighbor and you are going to say to him, "Your water quenches the thirst of many, and I am strong enough to carry it to them. May I take of it?" And you will go to another neighbor and you will say to him, "Your garden is very beautiful. There are meager gardens in the world, and mine not necessarily, but there is not enough for them in my garden to make the others beautiful. Will you give me of your seed so that I will make these beautiful, and I will carry that seed myself?" And believe me, my child, if they are working for the right they will be only too glad to give you of seed. But if they are working for themselves, and if they are making bargains with the God-consciousness, and they are working for exhibitionism, they will say, "Well, maybe you can have that. We do not want it." Well that seed will not grow, my child, because if it did they would have kept it. So you have the perfect right as a steward, or an over-steward, in the Universe, who sees water and fruit and beauteous seed sometimes going to waste, and whether it is or is not going to waste, you have the right to ask for it that some poor, sordid garden may be made beautiful. But be careful in asking that you, too, are not saying, "Behold what I can do!" Be very certain that you are not standing on the road with the seed in your hand and saying, "I wonder if I can use all this myself." No, be very certain to take just what you want to use for your garden and give away the rest. That is the law.

Q: *I am certain I can go to certain people and receive a reasonably small donation of, say, $100.*

Why not have a reasonably large figure in your own mind? Why limit it? Why set a figure on it? Get a figure in your own mind but do not go to them and lessen it. Let us hope every time that you solicit funding that you may receive more than you ask for. Do not limit a donor's capacity for giving by setting a figure in your own consciousness.

Tell them that the work is essential. When you go to these people show them the plan—a dignified plan—and say, "Now for this I need so much!" It need not be all that you want, or it may be more than you want. Simply show them a plan. A person gets interested in a plan much more than if you ask him for $200 to carry out something. You flatter him by taking him into your confidence—or what he thinks is your confidence. Begin to see the plan grow. Let him plant a little seed in the garden you have shown him. He would like to do it himself, but if he simply hands the seed to you, well, he has not much expression. When you go to these people and say, "I wish to do that," show them a hint of the garden. Let them see there is a garden. Now let them put in their own seed. Believe me, it will be a larger seed than if you limit their contribution. "I wish I could get $200 from them." That is the method of dealing with donors. Flatter them. Always go out with the belief that they are going to give you two or three packages of seed, not one. Go out with that, and always live up to an expectation greater than the man has got of himself. He is so startled and flattered that it has never ceased to work, and you will get good results.

Q: *Before I go out to solicit funds for my project should I make a demand of the Universe?*

Demand of the Universe that the donor shall give as largely as his capacity, and that you shall present to him the truth in which you believe in such a way that he will want to help with your project. In that way, you permit his conscience to grow larger and you permit your truth to grow larger, and when you say that it exemplifies your belief. Neither negate your own understanding nor negate your neighbor's understanding by creating a problem. A statement such as, "We are all anxious to frame such and so" inhibits it; but when you think to yourself rather, "I am going out with the definite belief that he is going to help," he is going to meet your request for help. State your belief first, following with what you want and why. And have no fear in your heart because if you have fear of rendering stewardship, the fear comes back on you and blots out the activity anyway, so ask for what you want with dignity.

Q: *Should I state directly that I need a donation of, say, $2000, and credit of several thousand more?*

That is an excellent presentation. You put your cards on the table and you let that resonate. If he only offers $200 take it— but as an installment, letting him know that you are only taking it as a little towards the lot. You sow the seeds as you go along. You sow the seeds of your own endeavor by the very method in which you shape your questions, so if he gives you only $200, keep the potential for more open. "Well, I am very grateful for it, but there is always the necessity for more," and show him the plan again, and in that way, you sow both the seed in his consciousness and in the Universe for your plan.

Never be afraid of asking, my child. It is no good asking in this way: "Oh, Lord, help me." Help you from what? "Lord, help me to help myself and bear the consequences of that that is alive." That is prayer. The man who says, "Oh God, forgive me." Forgive me for what? "Forgive me for taking up the experiences of today from yesterday's mistakes." The man who says and makes bargains with the Universe is no use at all! The man who says, "Protect me," why should he be protected? The man who says "God give me strength, vision and courage." That is prayer. Never be afraid to make the demand with all its implications. That is the way it comes back to you.

On Being a Shrewd Trader

If you do not seek to be a shrewd trader, then don't talk to me, my friend. I want to tell you very definitely that you have been given that and this to use. And I am not talking about commerce. I am talking about what is essential from you to me. If you are in business with me, my friend—let us put it like this: If we rub each other, if we have the same experience of soul, the rubbing goes on, you see, and on. If we do not have the same experience of thinking, one of us must go this way or that. If, therefore, my experience is not as great as yours, the only way my experience can grow is through the mistakes being corrected of my inexperience. It is not a question of shrewdness. It is a case of using that intelligence without sentiment, recognizing that you are God.

Working off the other fellow's energies is the only reason you are here. In the course of evolution, it is the one who struggles longest and finest who attains most. The selfish man is the Godful man. That is my attitude. The sentimentalist, my friend, will go to the well. The kind, tolerant personality, who has put shrewdness to one side, has insulted the hand of the Redeemer. There is no excuse to be made if you have the knowledge and do not use it. It is your responsibility to be as shrewd as you know how, which is to be slightly more shrewd than the other.

Aphorisms

The less time you give to an individual, the more respect he has for you.

No Man is kind to another unless there is a conscious or unconscious motive. He has his eyes widely open.

Cliques are the death of everything.

The pulpit is not the method of tomorrow.

The moment a man criticizes his partner, you may be certain there is something wrong with his own attitude.

When we begin to grumble and criticize and begin to be dissatisfied, you know very well there is something within ourselves that is causing that.

Every word that you say to me—every question that I bring from the roots of the unconscious—every time that you think of somebody else—is a nature of development.

There are many visionaries in the universe and unless they have construction as their motive, they destroy.

Defining your Point of View

A man has an idea and then sells it to you, and the rest of you follow that idea and out of that comes chaos. The Infinite has given you each an individual conception by which to work out the pattern of God.

Conscience

But what do you call a conscience, my friend? What is a conscience? Is it not one of these webs of deceit and conceit that men build around themselves to protect their sins and omissions from their neighbors?

On Jealousy

Jealousy is fear. What are you fearful of? Are you fearful that one will swallow the other so you are going to kill yourself swallowing the lot?

Being in a Fog

Man at times feels he is walking in a fog. All men do from time to time. If there were no fog, you would not enjoy the sunshine.

The Virtues of Silence

There is one rule in life: it is stewardship of the thing that you find yourself involved in. It is eminent stewardship. You are to render stewardship, give it. You give it in the hope that you create from that great fundamental effort. If something has come to you, with you, therefore, lies the responsibility. I do not think that by mentioning it within the community you do anything more than to distort it. Someone may say that is not good, another says this is not good. Beware that you can think a thing into disorder; always remember that. Apart from the fact that if you are going to become yourself possessor, so that the thing may be fundamentally clean and fine, with no untidy edges, you may as well begin to understand straightaway that there is nobody but yourself who can do this and that the only possible way in which you can render great stewardship is also with great silence, which brings wisdom.

What Seems Right to You, is Right

You ask me if something is proper and is it right? I cannot tell you, my friend. If I did I would be setting up myself as your counselor and I am only the interpreter on the highroad of life. If you ask me for the meaning of something I will tell it to you. I neither will guide you, counsel you, nor give you advice, and if I tell you what is right for you, I am making an infinite mistake.

It is right to do everything in the universe, if it is going to give to you pleasure and infinite joy. But you have to be sure of the rightness. There is no wrong in the universe, but there is negation of thinking. Therefore, what is right to you, what is essential to you, what you need and what you desire to do, if it seems right to you, is right. If you feel, therefore, the inclination to read a certain book, and you feel that it will please you and it will give you some little thought, read it by all means. But remember that while reading, it is the little points that you must interpret. There is no point too small, too mean, too insignificant to overlook, as it is by the little signposts that we find the great eternal road to rightness of understanding. Read what you will—that is good.

Do everything that you desire to do, providing the inner God says it is good and right and wise and good for you. That is right. There is no wrong, only in man's mind. But it is the negation of thought, which may produce the thing that man calls wrong; for that is the law. If you behave according to that law you do not break the laws of the people.

Millstones from the Past

Let us say that millstones from the past are around your neck. My friend, if the good God called you to the long journey tomorrow, what would you do? You would recognize that you had to let go, would you not? I am doing no more than beckoning a finger for freedom to you. Therefore, in the mind of thinking, I want you to think like this: Very well. These things have been handed on to you. They are a problem. In your case you need money. That is very definitely necessary. But you must get a freedom of thinking first, and then think to yourself, "What actually do I need?" and think, "What do I actually need that those belonging to me may not really suffer?" Count what you have in good health, count what you have in freedom of thought, count what you have in the blessings of your family and realize, my friend, that these are your only assets in life. It is surprising what such thought will do to you for your method of freedom.

And now, all right, these things have been, shall we say, a picture of your past but you are not carrying them into the future. Therefore, see—spend a little time with me alone, in your office or where you will—and let us see these things and tell to the universe that you place them there to be taken care of, to be made ready for the movement, since there is no standing still in the universe. Get the knowledge to you that every movement means movement of some nature, and that that movement can be in rhythm with your own thinking. See each one of these burdens of yours being converted into the little that will help you to freedom.

If you do definitely believe what I tell you, you then believe that the very food, the very clothing, the very necessities that you receive for your well-being, come to you through the force of the intimate direction that is received in the earth from the sun and the moon and the universe around you. That is definite. There is not even the rain for your crops—there is not even the metal within your ground—there is not the oil that has not been, shall I say, directed from without rather than from within. There is wisdom, direction and utility in this universe for you, and if you can therefore take hold of all these things and stand down in this universe and demand that they shall be one by one removed, then of a necessity you are beginning to free yourself bit by bit. Understand that all of mankind and you are an intrinsic part of the Greater Plan of the Universe.

On Forgetting the Past

The past is past. The things of the past have served their purpose. It is in the system of evolution that you move on. Man is the only one of God's creatures who drags the past around his neck. Do not think that the rest of evolution thinks of the pangs of yesteryear. Man would live so cleanly, so finely, with each other if he would only forget. If you could only ever manage to stop talking of what your fathers did and what your forefathers did, and take the good time to make good in the moment. Then there would not be the necessity today, the insecurity basis, which you will have to meet a little later. The past has been important. It has been useful. Throw the echoes of the past out into the universe with the greatest kindliness. Let them be useful to somebody else. They are the frills of yesteryear.

How You Progress

You make more progress when you see nothing at all—when you stand still. You only have this quiet conviction when you notice the progress in your daily life. Oh, my dear friend, the moment that you are able to say "yes" and to say "no", without "maybe so," "maybe not," "I think it may," "it could be," "it can be," "maybe it will"—these are the wasters of your energy. These are the comments that stifle your progress. "Yea" to the Universe, and it is filled with plenty for you. "Nay" and you stimulate someone else's "Yea".

You can only judge your progress by the strength within yourself. You can only judge your progress by the quiet exaltation that makes you trust the universal law and yourself as God-becoming. You can only judge your progress if you can have the conviction that the Universe in which you are and of which you are a unit, a part, is there for your becoming, that you owe it to duty and responsibility, but you are not here to move about in it and waste the hours; that you are here to identify yourself with it making for the Universe and the rightness of thinking, and that a million years hence you are doing the same thing by other universes; and that there is no end to this conception, but that it goes on and on and on and on, and that according to the rightness of your thinking today is the rightness of your thinking a million years hence. You have thought right up to this stage, or you would not be here in this state, that within you is the force and you will know how you progress not by your own lack of effort, but by your force of thought. But there is a difference. You will know also by your ability to say to a man, "It is—it is not." You will know also by the respect that is paid you by others. You will know by the unity and visible accents of every day that could not have happened last year.

For as you grow to grace within yourself, you cannot help but impress the other man with the change. It is nothing you say or you do but his own soul recognition saying to him, "That man has something I have not, and that cannot be idealism unless it has the conviction of doing and being." That is the only idealist I am interested in. The rest cause confusion— necessary in the process of evolution. Why be in the army of destructionists when there is need for real construction? I tell you, choose that you will look within yourself for guidance.

Open Yourself to Look Within

The problem of every individual is the shared difficulty you experience in opening yourself to look within. It is very often that you can see for other people. But you are always rather inclined to not look within, and it is necessary that one has an evaluation of self at all times. This cannot come in a hurry. It can only come over a process of time. But at the same time there is no doubt that if you truly desire to make an analysis of yourself, you must look within yourself so that you may be more and more aware of the help and the opportunity that surrounds you. It is not a process that can be entered into quickly. It is a process of watchful and careful criticism of oneself every day for a little while. It is a process of doing everything that is at hand to the moment and doing it cheerfully. It is a process of knowing what are the things within oneself—your aims. It is a process of not fooling one's own mechanism. That, of a necessity, although it sounds simple, is not always so. Men have spent many years looking within themselves for wisdom, and some with no success. Yet it is possible day by day to grow to a greater understanding of self—for only so does one grow to an understanding of the other fellow's point of view, as well enabling the realization that tolerance is the only asset that the human constitution can really work with. This comes only if one truly desires it, though it does not come quickly, and these introspections take time.

Many people are inclined to avoid knowing themselves. Many are inclined to call their motives by other names. One of the things that man must not do is be unfair or unkind or practice deception with himself. Many from an egoistic position are inclined to extol their better characteristics. It is always well to know that one is just as good as one can be as a day permits, as the experience of the day permits. Man must take stock of himself at all moments. Be certain that your impulses are understood by yourself. You cannot fool the self, and you cannot fool the spirit, but you can mislead yourself by giving to them names and titles, which are not truly theirs. We have all met the man who is inclined to exaggerate so much so until he begins to actually believe his exaggerations themselves. Self-deception is the easiest thing in the world to practice and the hardest to get away from. And if one is deceptive with oneself, then one cannot see and deal fairly or squarely.

On Being Fine and Fair

If you want to be fine and fair, my friend, you will do no less than be fine and fair. If you are going to look after yourself rightly, believe me the other fellow is not going to suffer. If you see that your purse is lined, if you have looked to that degree of well-being and well-thinking and thankfulness to the Universe, you will not allow your brother to starve. You will see that his purse is full in comparison to your own and to his method in life. Inasmuch as he has helped you, you help him to make himself what you are.

But do not take hold of your brother and put him on his two feet so that neither you nor he can move. Gently, you cannot leave hold of your brother that you have held him for so long. He may have become crippled, my friend, but you can gently, but firmly, raise him to his feet so that he knows the hour is coming that he may walk by the aid of his own staff. That is the law.

Feeling Overwhelmed

You cannot render good stewardship if the day overcomes you. The thing that you have to deal with is the "now." At all times it is the "now." It is not the four or five or six of the day. It is the bringing to the moment the best you have. And if you bring to this moment the best you have, of a sincerity and necessity the next moment is surely also taken care of. I cannot see that one should feel lost anywhere when overwhelmed with the day's activities. One may feel that one is doing very little, but if one has sincerely and honestly tried to do the best that the day has presented, there is no need to be hard on yourself and "become lost".

Egoism

A man without ego is the man who is not performing the just and right duties of Godship. Each man must have respect and strength of ego. But glorification of ego is the thing that I warn you to not overdo. Be that what you are. Inasmuch as you are, so God is realized within you. But let it be in health, in vigor, in aspiration and in achievement rather than in the sense of feeling pleased that your egocentricities are developing much more strongly. Let your achievements develop and your ego will take care of itself.

Confusion

There can be no growth if there is not growth out of mistakes. If you tell me, "I never have any confusion," I would not believe you. It is impossible not to be at times confused. It is impossible that we are always sitting in the sunshine. But when you are confused, sit down and say, "Now, what am I doing?" and take a look at it all. Or leave it for a moment, take your hands off it and it will clarify itself most perfectly. Every point that confuses you, take a look at it; see what is in it. See if it is right, not only for you but for the other fellow. If there is something in it you like, use it, but don't use it because somebody has presented it to you. Use it with your own intelligence. This is terribly important. This is the answer to every question. Use your own intelligence. This is the most difficult advice I have to give to any of you—to be intelligent for yourself. It is the easiest thing in the Universe— yet man refuses to use his own intelligence, to his detriment.

Responsibility to Children

You are responsible for bringing your children into the world. But I do not want you to wrap it around with sentimentality. Recognize this is the law. The soul desires to be born. There has been no accident in your life. There is naught accident in the universe—not anywhere. It is constructive and related in every aspect of it. These children have been souls desiring to be born. Sympathies, even protests, can bring them to your being. That movement of impulse that brings you to the conception of that body is your responsibility.

You decide to give them a beautiful temple in which they may live. So you help construct it with love and understanding. During the time that they are building that temple, you give them of the best you know. You give them as little "do not" as possible, but you do not achieve the "do" for them. When they are able to think for themselves, rightly or wrongly, whatever their thinking may be, and they reach that point in different stages, naturally, and in different states of education—when they are able to stand alone, my friend, they must stand alone. But as long as they are not able to take their place in the world of men, they are your responsibility. After that, when they are able to stand up and say, "We have our own wings. We fly," they cease to be your responsibility. That is the law.

The man who interferes willfully and willingly and conscientiously with the stream of another soul's becoming, is taking the responsibility upon himself of the ills and ailments of that irritation. But if we give the best we know, if we say, "this is the best I know for you. This I have done for you. Now, with what I have given you, take up your start and walk out," it is well. That is the law. Until the moment and time when the child is able to look after itself, it is the responsibility of one or the other parent—there is no doubt about that. Never mind what either parent has done to the other. That is not the child's responsibility. It came in with the full knowledge that the temple of that soul would be in a building process until it can go on to build for itself. That is the law.

An Observation on "Family"

No man in this Universe has come to me and said he is the son or daughter of that. What is family? Look back in the records of family and what have you got? Pretense—robbery—loot. Not one of you has the right to the claims that you proved. Must you live on your claims? I live on my right to be honest in this Universe, and if you cannot live by that I have no time for you. What does family mean? I tell you, my child, when I hear of all these families, that they have come from this and that, you cannot prove it. You may prove it through one generation, two generations, maybe three generations. You cannot be responsible and you cannot say what your grandfather has done. You cannot certainly say what your great-grandfather has done and was, and knowing the human attitude in life I can say that the most noble family has the greatest dung-heap. That is the attitude. A man is not a man because he happens to be born in the purple within a royal family. A man is a man because he is able to take your hand and look you in your eye and deliver to you personality and understanding, and if he has not that you have the right to throw him from your door.

On Giving Too Much of Oneself

There is one thing in the human concept you must also be aware of: When you throw yourself under the feet of the multitude, the multitude sometimes forget that they are trampling upon a human. There is a difficulty in giving too much. You may be too anxious to give too much of yourself, and the more you give of yourself the more the other fellow expects you to become the mat under his feet. But the moment you cease to be right there, the moment that you move your body from under his feet, he will know the initial change has taken place and from that moment he will respect you. From the moment he respects you, you are the master of the situation. And then bit by bit, bit by bit, you see yourself. This is the way the Universe helps you.

Thinking About the Other Fellow First

I am not definitely interested in many of the people you talk about. I have no interest whether you, as an individual in commerce, sink or fail. But I have the responsibility of God's creatures, to God's creature, that you are. I have walked this way before you. Even yet, the footsteps on the road that remain with my mistakes face me. I see them as mistakes in the light of greater experience. I cannot take your difficulties, but I can show you the map of them. I can see you thinking, and I know the inefficiency of thinking for the other fellow first. Believe me, if you think for yourself conscientiously, you will not do less for your neighbor. If you have not treated yourself with idealism, but with certainty and lack of sentimentality, I cannot trust you to know how to deal with your neighbor. That is all I say to you. Therefore, the thing begins, "What do I want to do—I the individual? I want to eliminate of these things from around my shoulders. I want to be up, to be doing. Not for money." No. If I thought it was for money, I would not be talking to you, "but for the essential good and the production of beauty, and also that I may live with those to whom I hold responsibility in the sight of happiness." That is your ideal.

First, last and always, you must realize you cannot be definitely constructive until you turn around and face your responsibilities. You may lose a lot in doing it, but you will lose no more than if you keep them around your neck. Meet your responsibilities and so you begin to set yourself free. And I do not mean you can ignore these things. I can, for example, look at my army, and I can see my generals, and I can see where my army is ill-fed and weak. Well, now, I cannot sit on the wall and wail for their weakness. No. I have got to think how I can best see that that contingent is fed. That does not mean that

I am going to get off the wall now and wail and say, "Woe is me that they are not fed." I have to be up and doing that there shall be no hunger within their midst. Do you see? That is the way. But I am not taking that to my bedroom with me, nor am I taking that to my business with me, nor to my friends. There it is. It is my responsibility. There is the first weakness to be dealt with the first starving man. I must leave the rest of the army. You carry on for a little while finding a solution. That is not ignoring, you see. It is recognizing. But whilst I am dealing with the first to be fed I am praying to God that the rest may be fed. Make the image of your responsibilities. Then look at them all and say, "Where is the weakness and which will stand longest?" Get a definite plan of thinking to yourself and get everything aligned that is around your neck.

Q: *Should I then continue to ask the Universe for guidance and help?*

I hope you are not merely going to talk to the Universe, because it may be too busy to listen to a gentle speech. I hope you are going to arrest it. My friend, are you not tired—are you not tired to the heart of the prayer to the universe? Are you not tired of the formula that is dead and dying—that contains no will of its own? There is no joy like going out unto the hilltop of your own being, and throwing your arms out and saying "This I need!" That is prayer. And the only difference between prayer and demand is that demand is stronger and prayer is usually mixed up in the minds of the people with the formula. The man who says for the first moment in his life, "God help me" has prayed earnestly.

Religion and Social Service

I am always suspicious, and you must forgive me when I say this, of anyone that is identified with religious education or the social service. I have always found in dealing with such minds that, however free they are, there is always in the eleventh moment an inability to see anything but one's own point of view. An artist I can always deal with, but the very title and the fact that he would in any sense unconsciously identify himself with it, would give to me the impression of saying, "A charming companion for dinners," but I have nothing to offer you as to his courage.

Man and His Body

Remember this: the good God, when he made man and put him upon this earth, intended that man should follow the rule—of the animal, in a way—gave man certain fruits of the land, certain foods. But man was not satisfied and in the very beginning he gave in to the yearnings of his physical appetite. The first appetite is a physical curiosity, which man followed to his own devastation. He felt that he must kill for the joy of eating, and if he must kill he must eat, and then must go on eating and eating. And now, generations of ancestors have eaten wrongly and laid up for you a nervous system which is truly not your own. You begin the world with it. Currently in your everyday life you eat here and you eat there, and sometimes if you saw what you were eating you would have a very great shock. A very great deal happens in your stomach which is a delicate, beautiful organism, lined and interlined with glands and the secretions of glands; and it comes in contact straightaway with condiments and with forceful food that not only shocks it but puts it out of any kind of working order. But the stomach does its best. Food has to pass through, after all, many inches—thirty-two feet of intestine. The intestine is lined, or the mucous membrane is lined, with secretions. All the secretions are doing their very best as well. But when one tiny little nerve gets out of order in one place, the whole thirty-two feet of nerve is affected.

Though the intestines also do their best, they become lined

with fecal matter. This fecal matter over the large area sets up its own disease, it sets up its own odors, and it lives on itself. The digestive tract does the very best it knows until bit by bit, sadly only the very tiniest passage remains open for the digestive tract, with the mucous membrane of the intestines—all usefulness of it gone as it has become lined, relined and interlined with fecal matter. Until you remove that fecal matter you can have no good digestion. You will have the inevitable amount of return of the chemical gases. You will have deflations, inflations, corresponding pains, lack of appetite, and, bit by bit, you will have a starved and poisoned nervous system. The sympathetic nervous system will break down; and then you will find the locomotive nervous system will begin to miss, as it would in your car or in your plane. You will immediately understand that something is wrong but you will go on abusing your body. So the first essential is to see that you cleanse that, and then get your bloodstream in order, and dare I suggest that you actually rest occasionally and take substances that will feed the nervous system and help cleanse the fecal matter from the intestines.

To clear the fecal matter, in the supply of the Universe the good God has given you in your fruits and vegetables not only all your starch and energies, but has given you all your lubricants and quick acting toxins; so if you will take something that is a preparation of spinach or green vegetables or the nettle that is not even looked at—these things contain 98% arsenic in the compound and these are the things that we overlook and ignorantly cook and boil them and throw the essence of them away. If you will take a tonic consisting of the nature of these greens, you will find that that will help you enormously and give to you a great deal of resistance and tolerance in the system.

On Sentiment

If you need and care for someone at the moment, that is well. If they be useful to you, keep them and watch them, and when their utility is over and you come to the conclusion that there is nothing more between you, then gently and firmly say, "Well, we have played along, but I can't any longer." This sounds harsh but if the time comes that you are continuing a relationship purely on sentiment—let sentiment go and let reason step in. You see, man is doing things based on sentiment, and he, in doing so, crushes the life out of the very one that he hopes to protect while literally killing himself. Sentiment is a dark pool in which there are many dangerous currents, and he who tries to swim in it may lose his life.

Intuition—the Language of the Soul

In this life you are taught but one language, and that is the language of defense. Every word that you utter in the ordinary sense of the word, from the moment you bid to your friend good morrow until you say good night, is not really true of you. Very few humans can dare to speak that which is the truth, and so we all live, as it were, behind a barrage of words. We do not do that when we become enlightened.

There is only one language that we may listen to, and that is the language of the soul. Now, the soul knows no fear, and the spirit needs experience and it has no fear. And it sees, long before the chemistry feels, what is good for you. And it sends out to you this soul language. But in the ordinary sense of the day you are disinclined to believe it and you are suspicious of it. You think it is your imagination. Well, what if it were? It is your original creative thinking force, and if it comes to you with an alertness, it comes to you with sanity and logic. You cannot disobey it because nothing—no man, no matter how highly paid he is—can give to you the advice that the soul logic can give as being best for you. And so, when you find this intuition coming up and being a part of you—a very vigorous part of you—obey it, because it is the language of the soul and contains for you the right element.

Fear

Fear is the death of mankind. If you would understand the great ennobling lesson of security, you would have no fear. Many of the inconsequent fears, which are the consequential ones, you carry over from every evolutionary process. Tell me a man's fear and I will tell you exactly through what evolutionary process he has achieved his state of humanity. Many of these fears are groundless, but the predispositions to them have been carried with you, and an insecurity in thinking has caused other little receptacles to spring up. Where there is fear, there is sickness. Where there is sickness there can be no health. Where there is fear there is no security. Fear is the thing that kills the human race. There is naught to fear, my friend, if one lives in security, but realize it is the predominating factor in all chaos, in all insecurity.

You make your life the harder. You have come into a universe of peace, of beauty. I do not blame the man who goes astray and never sees the beauty. I have always said—and will always continue to say—that the education of the child, or the lack of it, is the thing that causes the depths of insecurity. But it is never too late to overcome that. And if you will face the things that threaten you and say, "Well, here I am; what are they?" you will find that they are the little things, the little reticules containing these things in your own mind, placed there, maybe, or garnered by wrong thinking. And if a man has God, he has everything for the road that I would leave with you. And you neither say "if" or "but" or "I think" or "I try" or "maybe," but you get the glorious understanding of saying "no" and "yes"— "yea" and "nay." The sounds of them in the Universe alone are convincing.

On Writing

The brain, my child, nobody else can conceive. Nobody else can express himself in the same way as you can. That is the rationale for writing. Writing, after all, is a process of creation—the creation surely manifesting from your experience of living. If somebody wants your writing, it literally is a signpost that they believe in you, and if they believe in you it means that others in the world can believe in you. That is why you should write. Every time that one word—never mind the sentence—but every time that you write one word of sincerity you may be perfectly certain that one word of sincerity will strike somebody in the Universe. And if it has done that, it has brought good.

What you write is the bellows of your soul. Never mind whether it is flippant or joyous—never mind what it is—it is *you*. And you owe that responsibility to the Universe or the Universe would not be calling on you to do it. Write—certainly write. It releases you and it brings to you new ideas. Never mind about the technique and the style. The world is full of technique and style. That is why there is so little definite thinking. You cannot think of art today unless you think of something that you can put a form on it. You cannot think of writing but you think of beauteous words. What is the use? You have something to give, you have a picture to paint and you have a child that is born to yourself. If you can get these into the Universe, believe me that is not ego—it is utility.

On Criticism

If you live, as I want you to live, you will not have time for criticism, either from yourself, to yourself, or of other people. You see, you all live, do you not, saying, "Look at him." You must, however, look at yourself. If you examine yourself carefully and rectify your mistakes, believe me, no man's criticisms can hurt you because you have nothing to be criticized for. And if you go about criticizing yourself, then you are applying the stick to the shoulder just the same. "Behold in me the martyrdom, the self-pity, the self-glorification, the self-adulation." That is all that self-criticism is. Criticism from your friends you cannot stand—because your soul tells you that you deserve it. Give up criticizing and look in the mirror and see what you can do to take it away, and that applies also to the criticism of your neighbor. "If, after all, I am a law to myself, I am a law to myself" and men begin to recognize it. They have nothing to say if you are living rightly. That is the thing. You only get criticism from people who do not know you. If your friends criticize you, it is your own fault. They cannot be your friends. The people who do not know you must be aware of you and they must be afraid of you, and they must recognize your methods are strong.

Have you ever noticed the man that dares to stand up against criticism? A man can dare to stand alone because he has a firm conviction that, rightly or wrongly, he has his point of view. The bullies of life go around shouting, and then along comes one fellow who knows that he can take a beating with the courage of his convictions. It is strange that when a man does show that he can, there are no more fights. A man who can think for himself must be admired.

Law of the Universe

Man has long sought the law of the Universe. The greatest difficulty, my child, is not to *give* you the law—that is easy enough—but to make you understand it. I have given Man the law so many times, but he does not—and is not expected to—comprehend the meaning. Man feels very definitely that everything that he does he must get his hands on it.

Now: all thought, all creative material is born of the spirit. Spirit passes this desire to the soul and the soul to the mechanics of the body. So the child's first effort of drawing is his first aspect of telling you that he is trying to create God in his own image. Each one of you feels, however, that you must do it either with the expense of an awful amount of energy or time or material or organizing or beating yourself or that you must stupefy others. That is not the way at all. Look at the thing that you want to do. Ask yourself very definitely if it appeals to you to do. Is it something in which your demand, the Creator, can be interested? Has it got something in production that will definitely please you that you have taken a hand in it, or even that you have administered it? And look at it and see what is its use in the Universe, because you may as well recognize you are here not only for your own growth but that the evolution of the Universe shall undergo some change by your being here.

I do not care in the long run whether you sit still or whether you go on. Only, if you sit still, life unfortunately either throws you into confusion or throws you out, because life is so well ordered that you are not permitted by anything that you do to throw confusion into the beautiful symmetry of it all. So you really do confuse yourself and you can pass that confusion— just as any form of hysteria is passed in a community, so does your untrue or confused thinking confuse every issue with which you come into any form of understanding.

The law of the Universe, therefore, says think as the little child does; and then formulate your thinking around the creativeness. Do not do it if you are not interested, if you do not see its constructive reality. And do not give yourself to any cause, however lucrative or productive, unless you see its complete utility. Now, if it has something to offer you, that is utility. If it has cash value to offer you, if it has the furtherance of your plans or ideals, that is something to offer you. Now when you begin to do it, get your plans out. Let the thing, once it has become formulated, have its chance. It is a creation, and if it is, and has a reality, then it must live. Nothing happens in a hurry. If it does, it is abortive. Take your hands off it and allow it to live. If the thing is right and you see its use and you see your interest and it has utility and graciousness and construction it will live.

Man's Place in the Universe

Man is born here. I have attempted to manifest this so many times in various generations that it might be that Man gets tired of hearing it. This is a Universe not for self-preservation but for the preservation of self. There in one fundamental law that governs the beginning, the end, and all the intermediate stages of this Universe, and that law, greater than any other law that may be pronounced by any great psychologist, is the preservation of self. Now, I do not talk of the preservation of the body. We do little to care for the body, yet we are trying to continually preserve the bodily "us." I am talking to you at this moment of the law that you have come into this life to comprehend and to understand, and if you do not understand it in this life it is a law that you will find in every form of life until you have mastered it. I think every living human understands that law, in every process of evolution occurring in the forest, in the water, in the sky, in the unseen and the seen, and recognizes it. Yet the human himself does not recognize it in himself. This is the law of the preservation of self. It is the law of individual development. It is the law of the ego individualized.

Look at spring in a forest. Look at the bluebells or at any of the beauteous spring flowers. And notice the path of their beauty. Look at the trees. Look at the woods. Look at the meadows. Look at the sea. Look at the sea urchins. Look at the oyster. Look at any one form of life, and you will see what I mean. There is not a patch in the forest, but there would be if the flowers used the human intelligence. Each flower has taken from the God-consciousness of his Universe, irrespective of his brother, with aforethought to himself and his family, color, light, air, oxygen to his roots; and he has overcome every enemy until he has shown himself a beauteous thing in the face of the Universe. And his brother and his brother's brother are no less beauteous. Now, there has been no selfishness in that. The plan is complete. The pattern is woven beautifully.

Now, envision a beautiful carpet and let us put ten intelligent human beings down to weave a pattern in so many days. Well, in the first day they will want to know what the other fellow has done. They will probably have disagreed in the third day. Maybe one will have tired, and the other fellow will have left his work to help his neighbor on the fourth, and on the fifth his pattern will not be showing clearly; and on the sixth, when the overseer comes, there will be a thread dropped here and a stitch there, and maybe there will be one who has gone on sewing and has taken no notice but has done his work. Do you get my meaning? Unless each one of the intelligent ten individuals had seen his work clearly to do, and done it to the exclusion of all else, the beautiful pattern would not be finished.

If the flower taking the light of God had said, "I do think I am overshadowing my neighbor," the probabilities are that you would have a patch in the woodland, and you have given of your energy and your peace of mind and your work, and unfortunately, your innermost thoughts and yourself, and what have you kept? The squeezed sponge.

But the other man has profited. He has been charming and kind. There is nothing you can lay at his door. He has listened to you. He has absorbed from you. He has even enthused you. And after a little while you are destroyed, and he has taken all your activity and he has put it into action. In other words, you have been so anxious that the flowers of the forest should look beautiful that when it came to your blooming, you had given all to them. I do not preach a selfish gospel, but I do tell you it is only the selfish man who makes the Universe—and by that I do not mean the petty man, the man who is grasping for himself, but I mean the man who sees a road and sees his original force and thought and puts it into activity.

The Difference Between the Spirit and the Soul

The compound that you call anything of God's—whether it is the stone or whether it is mankind—contains three exquisite forces. One is the chemistry, or the externals, which we see. The soul is exactly as the lining to the beautiful jewel. It partakes of the chemistry of the body and it partakes of the beauty of the spirit. We confuse soul and spirit, but the soul is the wrapping of the spirit, which is in its own country or comes into its own development at the state of death, as you call it. The soul is as biologically necessary to the spirit as is the body. But after the biological change that you call death, the soul has its development in greater fullness taken care of. The spirit, whether it is today, a million years hence, whether it is in the sun, in the moon, in the human contact, or in the stone that you kick—that spirit is inviolate and always perfect, but growing through struggle and experience to greater perfection. Remember there is always perfect—perfection in the spirit. But the spirit itself seeks these greater clothes and changes that it may know all perfection. And it is to ultimate perfected consciousness that our whole journey and the journey of all satellites—all life—is going. Not all spirit is in the same state of consciousness, but all spirit is perfect. Therefore, the soul must be, since it is almost wrapping the spirit—it is a vehicle for spirit, and comes into its fuller growth as a vehicle of itself in that change after death when the body is dissipated and goes back to help in the evolution of other grades of living. It takes on and is the vehicle of spirit.

The soul is individual, seeking—the spirit is individual. The soul that enwraps it belongs to it. It is individual but attached very definitely to the spirit. It is the casing if you like. But the body can be changed, for the body is but the mechanics of the moment, which protects the soul and permits the spirit through the soul, because the soul is between—it permits it so that the mechanics be used. From absorption of spirit to the mechanics of the body, the soul operates between the two. Soul and spirit go hand in hand. The mechanics of body can be picked up in any formation of matter. The body is not individual. But the soul and spirit are. The spirit *is* the God-essence. It is the essence of God growing and expanding. It is the spark of divinity that is related to the whole of life and therefore to the whole of God.

Remember the still small voice—as humanity calls the conscience—is nothing, after all, but the voice of the soul. And the spirit demands that the soul shall pass this experience through to the body that it may grow and achieve. Your consciousness participates in both the soul and spirit. The soul as I tell you is the casing or the inner case that holds the perfect jewel. One cannot contact soul without contacting spirit also.

You and the Universe

God is and God Becomes. The Universe will flow through any avenue, irrespective of what that avenue is, because the Universe is the breath of God. You are just one of the cells. Injure one of the brain cells, here, my child, and what happens? Confusion, for the time being. Sooner or later another brain cell will take, perhaps. That is a therapy that you do not even understand yet. But the whole confusion, the whole flow is not going to stop though confusion can be the result. Now, it is not what is in your mind. It is what flows through your mind. So that God is and God is becoming.

You have got to be on the road. The probabilities are that many times, having been brought up to beat your brow and hide your head and call yourself a miserable sinner, that you will step back onto that piece of ground. Nobody is going to cut out and fashion that new road for you. That is your job. And meanwhile, it will be very often useful for you to step back into the misery, the complexities of human understanding, until that other road is prepared. Now do not be ashamed of it if you fall back. That is your safeguard. Do not be afraid to fall from grace. In fact, fall very definitely. Do not throw yourself; however, if you find yourself on the ground, pick yourself up and take a rest before you dig into the new road. Have no compunction about making mistakes because they are the clods of earth of the new road. Do not beat yourself while expecting there is going to be a miracle. There will not be a miracle but there will be very definite work. It is an uphill struggle. You may well tell yourself, "My troubles only began the moment I began seeking for knowledge." That, of necessity, must be true as long as we live in a state of conscious frustration. Accept it! The moment you step out and become an individual consciousness, the eyes of the world are upon you. Every shaft of criticism is directed to you. But after a little while you grow immune to pain and do not mind the shafts. You may even grow arrogant with success. You cannot be too great for God's liking. You cannot be too important. Do realize that you are an avenue, after all—the breath of God as well as God-Becoming. Now, if you slip and fall and fall away and find yourself in a miserable wilderness occasionally, this is the best sign because if it did not seem like misery and a wilderness you would never have realized you had deviated off the correct road. It is only when you feel pain that you really realize you had been making any progress whatever. If you had not been making progress, you would not have noticed when you slipped back.

God takes care of you if you are doing absolutely your best each day. Divine protection is the result. If you do the best you know how today—never mind about tomorrow morning, saying, "I wish I had known." That has nothing to do with it. Tomorrow morning will be out—it is in the womb of time, unborn, and yesterday is within yesterday's ten thousand years. This moment comes—so long as you use the moment. Because you use this moment all the other moments will be used well, doing the best you can. Just do your very best, and that is all. Nothing else. Hold the philosophy of the Universe as doing the best you can with the moment of time that is here, now. Not a hundred years hence, not even ten minutes hence, because ten minutes hence is still out a thousand years. But now, this very moment.

If that is well with you, all is well. Now, if you want to play in this moment or you want to work in it, whatever you do—do it! But do not be thinking about it and wishing you could and not knowing how. Do! Do! Do!

Benediction

Now, my friend, may the blessing of the Universe be with you; but above all things, may the security of the Universe be engendered in that blessing. May the Infinite keep you in peace—gracious, tranquil peace, till we meet again. And if we do not meet again, remember that the blessing of my understanding goes along the road of life with you until that moment and time when you shall recognize your own security.

BOOK ONE

Call Me Lucifer

INDEX OF PASSAGES

BOOK TWO

Lucifer's Compendium of Guidance

INDEX OF PASSAGES

More from

Afterworlds Press

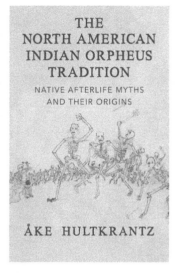

9 781786 771926